T0274873

BIBIMBAP

BIBIMBAP

and other Asian-inspired
rice & noodle bowl recipes

with recipes by
LOUISE PICKFORD

with photography by IAN WALLACE

RYLAND PETERS & SMALL
LONDON • NEW YORK

Senior Designer Toni Kay
Senior Editor Abi Waters
Creative Director Leslie Harrington
Editorial Director Julia Charles
Head of Production Patricia Harrington

Indexer Vanessa Bird

First published in 2023 by
Ryland Peters & Small
20–21 Jockey's Fields
London WC1R 4BW
and Ryland Peters & Small, Inc.
341 East 116th Street
New York NY 10029
www.rylandpeters.com

Text © Atsuko Ikeda, Jackie Kearney,
Kathy Kordalis, Jenny Linford,
Uyen Luu, Louise Pickford and
Ryland Peters & Small 2023
Design and photography © Ryland
Peters & Small 2023

Note: Some recipes in this book have
been previously published by Ryland
Peters & Small. See page 160 for full
text and photography credits.

ISBN: 978-1-78879-555-5

10 9 8 7 6 5 4 3 2 1

Printed and bound in China

A CIP record for this book is available
from the British Library. CIP data from
the Library of Congress has been
applied for.

NOTES
• Both British (metric) and American
measurements (imperial plus US
cups) are included; do not alternate
between the two within a recipe.
• All spoon measurements are level
unless specified otherwise. Note that
a level tablespoon (tbsp) is 15 ml and
a level teaspoon (tsp) is 5 ml.
• All eggs are medium (UK) or large
(US), unless specified as large, in
which case US extra-large should be
used. Uncooked or partially cooked
eggs should not be served to the very
old, frail, young children, pregnant
women or those with compromised
immune systems.
• Ovens should be preheated
to the specified temperatures.
We recommend using an oven
thermometer. If using a fan-assisted
oven, adjust temperatures according
to the manufacturer's instructions.
• When a recipe calls for the grated
zest of citrus fruit, buy unwaxed fruit
and wash well before using. If you can
only find treated fruit, scrub well in
warm soapy water before using.

FSC
MIX
Paper | Supporting
responsible forestry
www.fsc.org FSC® C008047

CONTENTS

INTRODUCTION

A meal in a bowl. I don't know about you but I know for sure that I prefer to eat almost all foods in a bowl. Bowls give ingredients structure and tend to be nourishing, comforting, hearty, healthy, satisfying, dynamic, colourful and idiosyncratic. Maybe it is the comfort angle or perhaps the idea of delving under different ingredients to see what lies beneath that makes them so inviting. Whatever it is, I'm definitely not alone in this. There is a long and rich history of serving a meal in a bowl and it is to Asia that we look for this.

The origin of the bowl as a vessel can be traced back to ancient times. The long history of the bowl combined with the importance of balance in every aspect of life in Asian cultures, led to foods being served together in one bowl; the ying and yang if you like. Even today, Asians use bowls more than any other nation and whatever is served at a meal, is eaten from a bowl.

Throughout Asia many dishes are named after the bowl in which they are served, such as Japanese donburi, Korean dolsot, Chinese gaifan, Vietnamese bun cha, Japanese ramen or Thai (or more accurately Buddhist) buddha bowl. This highlights the importance and their significance within each culture.

Where this differs slightly is with a Korean dish known as bibimbap, named after the ingredients rather than the bowl itself. Bibimbap is composed of 'bibim' meaning 'to mix things together' and 'bap' meaings 'rice'. So put together it is as simple as 'a bowl of ingredients with rice'. There are many different types of bibimbap in Korea all with very specific identities, and these are not limited to a special occasion or celebration, but served everyday as a family meal.

THE BOOK

The aim of bowl food is to provide a nutritious and well balanced meal in just one dish, with carbs providing the building blocks to which we add everything else. Protein will come from meat, fish or vegan products, such as tofu, tempeh or seitan. Vegetables will provide vitamins and minerals. Texture is just as important, so seeds or nuts are often used. Flavours must be balanced, and the use of soy sauce with either vinegar or lime is common along with sugar or honey. Sesame is used for umami richness.

Because rice or noodles make up the base of each bowl, toppings are packed full of rich flavours, especially from sauces and dressings to give balance. I believe it is this that makes Asian dishes so perfect for being served this way. If you think about the flavours that define Asian cooking, big flavours are prominent – soy sauces, earthy spices, intense citrus and vinegary flavours, pungent herbs, fiery chillies/chiles and rich coconut sauces.

Within each chapter you will find both rice and noodle bowls, inspired from dishes served throughout Asia, along with some that have been given a new, more contemporary twist. There is definitely a fusion element to the recipes, as I feel this is so much part of how we think and feel about our food today. I have tried to include recipes from all over Asia – from Korea, Japan, China, Indonesia, Thailand, Malaysia and Vietnam – to celebrate this wonderful way of eating.

Rice

Wherever we look for inspiration, it all begins with the carbohydrate. In this book rice and noodles make up the majority of carbs and they are as integral to Asian food culture as bread is to traditional Western cuisine.

Rice can be white, brown, red or black. Long-grain, jasmine, medium-grain, short-grain or sticky. Each recipe includes a particular type of rice to give that dish its balance of texture, flavour and

appearance, but overall it is not definitive and you can always substitute this with a different rice, perhaps due to preference, diet or even availability.

Raw rice always contains a dormant bacteria known as bacillus cereus and if rice is not prepared, cooked and chilled correctly it can be unsafe to eat. According to food scientist Harold McGee, to avoid food poisoning, cooked rice should either be eaten soon after cooking while still hot or cooled quickly and then kept refrigerated. You should also keep cold rice refrigerated until ready to either eat or reheat. The use of acidic ingredients in rice salads (or dishes such as sushi) helps prevent bacteria growing, making salads safe, which is why we add a dressing in each recipe. If you are reheating rice, this should be done from chilled and should be done only once.

I also recommend you follow the cooking instructions on each individual packet of rice.

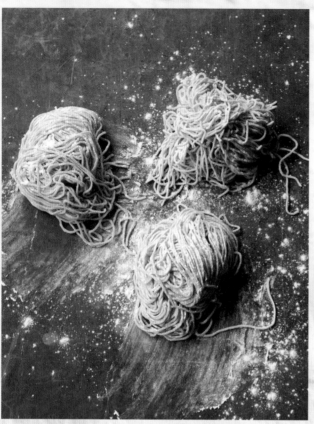

Noodles

Throughout Asia noodles are mostly served as one-pot dishes in soups, salads and stir-fries, providing the carbohydrate element of each dish, which we can again build on with the inclusion of vegetables, meat and fish. You will recognize many of the classic dishes, such as Japanese ramen and udon, and Thai or Vietnamese noodle salads.

As with rice, each recipe suggests a type of noodle in order to offer variety, texture, colour and flavour. You can vary this if you want, but always follow the cooking or rehydration instructions on each packet. Unlike rice, noodles are safer when it comes to cooling for use in salads, but always use best practices when serving cold noodles.

This really is a celebration of Asian bowl food, a collection of mouthwatering dishes for any occasion designed to both satisfy appetites and add a sense of wellbeing to our culinary world.

GLOSSARY OF UNUSUAL INGREDIENTS

Daikon – or mooli – is a winter radish grown throughout its native East Asia. Also known as Japanese or Chinese radish, it is widely available. Traditional red radish can be substituted.

Dashi – is a Japanese stock. Dashi powder is a convenient shortcut to making it, similar to a stock cube. It is available from Asian food stores. Fish stock can be substituted as a last resort.

Edamame – are immature soybeans eaten mainly in Japan. The little green beans, similar to baby broad/fava beans in appearance, are encased in a 5 cm/2 in. long shell and require shelling. More widely available frozen in the shell, you can now buy ready shelled beans in some large supermarkets or Asian stores.

Fermented soybean paste (doenjang) – is a Korean paste, similar to Japanese miso. It has a stronger flavour than its Japanese cousin, so is generally used in smaller quantities. It is available from online stores. Miso can be substituted, but add a dash of dark soy sauce for extra depth of flavour.

Galangal – is a rhizome related to ginger. It is similar in appearance to ginger but has a thinner, paler skin. It is difficult to pinpoint its exact flavour, but there are hints of ginger, pepper and even lemon. It is widely used throughout Asia and is a native of Indonesia. Ginger can be used instead. Galangal is available from specialist grocers or Asian stores.

Gochugaru – is the Korean name for red chilli/chili powder, 'gochu' meaning 'chilli 'and 'garu' meaning 'powder'. It is made from roughly ground dried chillies/chiles with an earthy red colour. Used extensively in Korean dishes, it has a slight smoky, fruity-sweet note to it with a high-powered kick. Available online, but regular chilli powder can be used instead.

Gochujang – is a Korean chilli/chili paste made with malted barley and gochugaru (amongst other things) giving it a distinctive hot, sweet/sour flavour. It is available from online stores and is pretty much essential if cooking any type of Korean dish.

Japanese mayonnaise – is typically made with egg yolks and is flavoured with rice wine giving it a rich depth of flavour. It is drizzled over certain Japanese dishes such as sushi and omelettes. Available from Asian stores or online. Regular mayonnaise can be substituted.

Ketjap manis – is a thick sweet soy sauce used extensively in Indonesian dishes.

Mirin – is a rice wine from Japan. It is similar to sake but is lightly sweetened giving it a more syrupy consistency.

Nashi pear – is a type of Asian pear that actually resembles an apple, with its pale green/brown skin. The flavour is very much pear and the flesh crisp and white. Available from specialist stores.

Palm sugar/jaggery – made from a variety of palm trees that grow in Africa and Asia. Slightly less sweet than other sugars, it has a delicate caramel flavour and is integral to Southeast Asian cooking. Available from Asian stores, it is sold in small discs that are grated before being used.

Sake – is a Japanese wine made by fermenting rice. It has a relatively high alcohol content. It can be used in cooking, as well as served hot or chilled as a delicious drink. It is widely available.

Shaoxing wine – is Chinese rice wine used in Chinese cooking. It is made from glutinous brown rice and has an earthy, nutty flavour. Although you could use another type of rice wine, Shaoxing has a superior flavour. Available from Asian stores.

Shrimp paste – is a dried and fermented fish paste with an intense, rather unpleasant gone-off fish smell. However once cooked in dishes it gives the food a wonderful depth of flavour. It is, if you like, the essence of Southeast Asian cooking. Once opened it needs to be stored in the fridge and used within 1 month.

Szechuan peppercorns – are in fact Chinese coriander, but as they are normally used in the same way as peppercorns they have become known as such. They have a delightful aromatic lemony flavour. Widely available.

Tamarind paste – is made from the pod-like fruit of the tamarind tree indigenous to tropical Africa. It has a distinctive sweet/sharp lemon flavour adding a subtle sharpness to savoury dishes. It is widely available in Asian stores.

Wasabi paste – is made from the root of a Japanese plant similar to horseradish. It is pale green in colour with a hot 'kick' to it. It is always served with sushi but makes a lovely addition to salad dressings. Widely available.

EASY DOES IT

The most well-known Korean dish, this humble rice
bowl is traditionally topped with all sorts of vegetables,
marinated meat (usually beef), a fried egg, a sprinkle
of sesame and a dollop of gochujang sauce. My take is
a lighter vegetarian version with 7-minute boiled eggs,
rather than fried, but super tasty nonetheless.

BIBIMBAP-Y BOWL

For the pickled carrots, stir the vinegar, sugar, salt
and 250 ml/1 cup water together in a saucepan over
a medium heat to dissolve the sugar. Set aside to cool,
then add the carrot and stand for 1 hour to pickle.
Drain the carrot from the pickling liquid before serving.

Cook the rice for 12 minutes in a saucepan of boiling
water. Drain, then remove from the heat and stand,
covered, for 5 minutes.

For the shiitake, heat a frying pan/skillet to a medium
heat, add the sesame oil, then the mushrooms and sauté
for a few minutes. In a bowl, mix the other ingredients
and pour into the mushrooms. Cook for another minute,
then remove from the heat and set aside.

For the spinach, blanch the spinach leaves until just
wilted, refresh in iced water, drain and squeeze dry.

For the gochujang sauce, combine all the ingredients
in a bowl and set aside.

Sauté the mooli and garlic in the sesame oil in a frying
pan/skillet over a low heat until just tender. Season to
taste and set aside.

Season the cucumber ribbons with the chilli powder
and some salt and set aside.

To serve, divide the rice among individual serving bowls,
add the kimchi, pickled carrots, shiitake and spinach on
top. Top each with a boiled egg half and serve hot with
the gochujang sauce drizzled over.

400 g/2 cups short-
grain brown rice,
rinsed
250 g/9 oz. mooli/
daikon, julienned
on a mandoline
1 garlic clove, crushed
1 tablespoon sesame
oil
1 cucumber, shaved
into ribbons
2 teaspoons smoked
chilli/chili powder
2 eggs, boiled for
7 minutes
80 g/3 oz. kimchi,
chopped
salt

PICKLED CARROTS
60 ml/¼ cup rice wine
vinegar
55 g/¼ cup caster/
granulated sugar
2 teaspoons salt
1 large carrot,
julienned on
a mandoline

FRIED SHIITAKE
1 tablespoon sesame
oil
200 g/7 oz. shiitake
mushrooms
2 tablespoons tamari
or soy sauce
2 tablespoons sake
1 tablespoon rice
vinegar
1½ teaspoons brown
sugar

WILTED SPINACH
200 g/7 oz. fresh
spinach

GOCHUJANG SAUCE
2 tablespoons
gochujang
1 tablespoon rice wine
vinegar
1 tablespoon soy sauce
1 teaspoon sesame oil
2 teaspoons roasted
sesame seeds
2 teaspoons Korean
rice malt syrup

Serves 4

This fresh and zesty Vietnamese noodle soup is packed with flavour from the chillies/chiles and lime leaves and makes a perfect quick and easy lunch.

PRAWN, PEA & PEA SHOOT SOUP

Soak the noodles in a bowlful of hot water for 20–30 minutes until softened. Drain well, shake dry and set aside.

Put the stock, onion, garlic, chillies, lime leaves, galangal and lemon grass in a saucepan set over a medium heat and bring to the boil. Simmer gently for 10 minutes until the soup is fragrant, then strain the stock through a fine-mesh sieve/strainer into a clean saucepan.

Stir in the fish sauce, lime juice and sugar, and set over a medium heat. Add the celery and tomatoes and simmer for 5 minutes. Add the prawns and peas, and simmer for a further 2–3 minutes, until the prawns are just cooked through.

Divide the noodles between bowls and pour over the soup. Serve topped with pea shoots and herbs.

350 g/12 oz. dried rice stick noodles

1.25 litres/2 pints chicken stock

1 small onion, sliced

4 garlic cloves, roughly chopped

2 red bird's eye chillies/chiles, pounded

6 kaffir lime leaves, pounded

2.5-cm/1-in. piece fresh galangal, sliced and bruised

2 lemon grass stalks, trimmed and bruised

3 tablespoons fish sauce

2 tablespoons freshly squeezed lime juice

1 tablespoon grated palm sugar

2 celery sticks, sliced

2 tomatoes, peeled, deseeded and diced

500 g/7½ cups (about 50) raw prawns/shrimp, peeled and deveined

150 g/3 cups peas

a handful of pea shoots

a handful of fresh herbs, such as perilla leaves and coriander/cilantro

Serves 4

Nasi goreng is a classic Indonesian rice dish that can be made with chicken or beef, or as a vegetable dish. It is most commonly served for breakfast in Indonesia, but is equally good as a lunch or supper dish.

NASI GORENG CHICKEN

Make the chilli paste. Place the ingredients in a pestle and mortar and grind to make a fairly smooth paste. This can also be done in a small blender.

Heat 2 tablespoons of the oil in a wok or large frying pan/skillet, and fry the spice paste over a medium heat for 1–2 minutes until softened and aromatic. Add the sliced chicken and stir-fry for 2–3 minutes until lightly browned. Then add the prawns and stir-fry for 2 minutes.

Add the rice along with a little extra oil if needed. Stir well, then add the soy sauce and ketjap manis and continue to stir-fry for a further 1–2 minutes until the rice is heated through and evenly browned. Keep warm.

Shallow-fry the eggs in 1 cm/½ in. of vegetable oil for 2 minutes until the whites are cooked through and the yolks are cooked but still runny.

Divide the rice between bowls and top each one with a fried egg. Garnish with tomatoes, cucumber, onion flakes and coriander and drizzle with the chilli paste.

2–3 tablespoons vegetable oil, plus extra for shallow frying

500 g/1 lb. 2 oz. skinless boneless chicken thighs, thinly sliced

250 g/9 oz. small raw prawns/shrimp, peeled and deveined

800 g/1¾ lb. cooked long-grain rice, cooled and chilled

2 tablespoons light soy sauce

1 tablespoon ketjap manis

4 eggs

chilli/chili sauce, to serve

RED CHILLI PASTE
4 large red chillies/chiles, sliced
2 teaspoons shrimp paste
2 garlic cloves, roughly chopped
4 shallots, thinly sliced

GARNISH
sliced tomatoes
sliced cucumber
crispy onion flakes
coriander/cilantro leaves

Serves 4

This is one of the most comforting dishes you will ever have. It is simply chicken and egg simmered in an umami-rich sauce atop some freshly cooked rice. If you want to eat in true Japanese fashion, put down your knife and fork and use chopsticks. The secret is to start from the bottom, digging in to get chunks of rice to mix with the toppings and you will have perfectly balanced mouthfuls.

CHICKEN & EGGS on rice

First, make the dashi. Place the kombu in a large saucepan with 1 litre/quart water and leave to soak for at least 30 minutes. After 30 minutes, start to gently bring the water to the boil over a medium–high heat. Just before it reaches boiling point – when small bubbles appear at the bottom of the pan – remove the kombu and continue heating. Once boiling, turn the heat off and sprinkle the katsuobushi into the kombu dashi. Leave to brew for 2 minutes, letting the flakes sink to the bottom of the pan. Strain the dashi through a muslin/cheesecloth or paper towel-lined fine-mesh sieve/strainer, letting it drip through.

Combine 180 ml/¾ cup of the dashi with the brown sugar, mirin and soy sauce in a medium frying pan/skillet and stir to dissolve the sugar. Bring to the boil, then add the onion and diced chicken. Turn the heat down to medium and simmer for 7 minutes, uncovered.

Meanwhile, break the eggs into a large bowl and lightly beat. Transfer to a pourable jug/pitcher. When the chicken is cooked and the onion is softened, pour the beaten eggs into the pan, starting from the middle and pouring towards the outside edges in a circular, spiral motion.

As soon as all the eggs have been added, shake the pan gently to create a marbling effect between the eggs and the seasonings. Reduce the heat to low and simmer for 2 minutes to soft-cook the eggs, then remove from the heat.

Portion the cooked rice into serving bowls and flatten slightly. Top with half the egg and chicken mixture each. Sprinkle the bowls with spring onion and tear up the nori sheet on top for some extra flavour. Serve with pickled vegetables for a refreshing crunchy taste, if you like. Serve while the eggs still have a melting, soft consistency.

2 teaspoons soft light brown sugar
2 tablespoons mirin
2 tablespoons soy sauce
1 onion, diced across the grain
2 skinless boneless chicken thighs, diced into small pieces
3 large/US extra-large eggs

KOMBU & KATSUOBUSHI DASHI
10 g/¼ oz. (5 x 10-cm/2 x 4-in.) piece of kombu
20 g/¾ oz. katsuobushi (bonito flakes)

TO SERVE
400 g/3 cups cooked white Japanese rice
1 spring onion/scallion, thinly sliced
1 sheet of dried nori seaweed
pickled vegetables (optional)

Serves 2

NOTE: You will not need all of the dashi for this recipe. Any leftover will keep in the refrigerator in a sealed container for up to 3 days.

This is one of the top five most popular donburi dishes in Japan. It is basically a bowl of rice topped with seasoned, very thinly sliced beef and onion. It's simple to make and hits the spot magically when hunger strikes. Here, tomato has been added to the traditional recipe for an extra layer of umami and a touch of colour.

SIMMERED BEEF & TOMATOES on rice

Slice the sirloin steak as thinly as possible (see tip below) and set aside.

Combine the sake, soy sauce, mirin and brown sugar with 100 ml/ scant ½ cup water in a saucepan and bring to the boil.

Add the sliced beef, the onion and ginger to the pan and bring to the boil again. Skim off any scum that comes off the surface of the beef. Reduce the heat to low-medium and simmer for 5 minutes, uncovered.

Add the tomato and simmer for another 10 minutes, carefully peeling away then discarding the tomato skins as they soften and start to separate from the flesh.

Portion some cooked rice into serving bowls, then top with the beef and tomato mixture. Add all the cooking juices so that the rice can absorb the flavours. Sprinkle with shichimi and enjoy.

TIP ON THINLY SLICING MEAT: The easiest way to thinly slice a large piece of meat is to wrap it in clingfilm/plastic wrap and freeze for about 2 hours for a thickness of about 10 cm/4 in., or a shorter time if the cut is thinner. You want the meat partially frozen, so the outside is firm and the inside is still soft. The texture should almost be the consistency of cured meat, rather than still frozen. This firmness allows it to be sliced much more thinly. Unwrap the meat and thinly slice across the grain with a sharp carving knife for the most tender bite. Leave the partially frozen meat at room temperature for 30 minutes to thaw out a little before using, or place back in the freezer for when next needed.

250 g/9 oz. sirloin steak

50 ml/3½ tbsp sake

2½ tablespoons soy sauce

2 tablespoons mirin

1 tablespoon soft light brown sugar

½ large onion, cut into 1-cm/ ½-in. wedges

5 g/⅛ oz. fresh ginger, peeled and cut into thin strips

1 large tomato, cut into quarters

TO SERVE

400 g/3 cups cooked white Japanese rice

shichimi (Japanese spice mix)

Serves 2

Making your own black bean sauce rather than using ready-made gives a far lighter result, especially as it is so often served with vegetables. You can soak or wash the black beans if you like, but I prefer to cook them as they come for added saltiness in the dish.

SWEET POTATO NOODLES
with broccoli in black bean sauce

Cook the noodles by plunging them into a large saucepan of boiling water. Return to the boil and cook for 1 minute until al dente. Drain well, refresh under cold water and shake dry. Set aside.

Next make the sauce. Whisk together the doenjang paste, sake, mirin, vinegar, soy sauce and sesame oil until smooth, then stir in the black beans. Set aside.

Heat the peanut oil in a wok or frying pan/skillet set over a medium heat and fry the ginger for 10 seconds until fragrant. Add the onion and stir-fry for 1 minute, then stir in the broccoli and continue to stir-fry for 1 minute, adding 1 tablespoon cold water, until the broccoli is a vibrant green.

Add the sauce and cook for 2 minutes until the broccoli is tender. Finally add the noodles and stir until heated through.

Serve in bowls garnished with toasted sesame seeds.

300 g/10 oz. sweet potato noodles
3 tablespoons peanut oil
5-cm/2-in. piece of fresh ginger, peeled and thinly sliced
1 red onion, sliced
250 g/4 cups broccoli florets
sesame seeds, toasted, to garnish

BLACK BEAN SAUCE
2 tablespoons doenjang (Korean bean paste)
125 ml/½ cup sake
60 ml/¼ cup mirin
2 tablespoons rice wine vinegar
2 tablespoons dark soy sauce
2 teaspoons sesame oil
3 tablespoons fermented black beans

Serves 4

Being landlocked, Laos makes best use of its many rivers and the fish that thrive there. This is typical of the type of fish soup that is eaten daily in Laos. Traditionally, the stock would be flavoured with a ham hock.

VERMICELLI SOUP with river fish

Preheat a stovetop ridged grill pan over a medium heat until it's smoking hot. Arrange the shallots cut-side down in the pan along with the garlic cloves and chillies. Char-grill for 5 minutes, turn over and cook for a further 5 minutes until everything is well charred.

Place the gammon in a large saucepan with 3 litres/quarts cold water, the charred vegetables, the galangal, kaffir lime leaves and fish sauce. Set over a high heat and bring to the boil. Simmer gently for 1½ hours, skimming any scum from the surface. Carefully remove the gammon, discard the skin and cut the meat into shreds. Set aside.

Soak the noodles in a bowlful of hot water for 20 minutes until softened. Drain well and arrange on a platter with the papaya, bamboo shoots, cabbage and snake beans.

Return the shredded meat to the stock, add the fish and simmer gently for 2–3 minutes until the fish is cooked.

Serve the soup from the pan so everyone can help themselves to the noodles, vegetables, herbs and other garnishes.

4 Asian shallots, halved
4 garlic cloves (skin on)
4 large red chillies/chiles
1 kg/2 lb. smoked gammon knuckle
5-cm/2-in. piece fresh galangal, peeled and sliced
6 kaffir limes leaves, pounded
2 tablespoons fish sauce
250 g/9 oz. dried rice vermicelli
100 g/½ small green papaya, peeled and shredded
50 g/⅓ cup drained and sliced bamboo shoots (optional)
125 g/¼ Chinese cabbage, thinly sliced
50 g/5–6 snake beans, trimmed and thinly sliced
250 g/9 oz. river fish fillets, such as trout or perch

TO SERVE
2 limes, cut into wedges
fresh chillies/chiles, chopped
fresh Thai basil leaves

Serves 4–6

For me what distinguishes Korean meat dishes from other East Asian dishes is the use of their very identifiable chilli paste or gochujang. It has a slight yeasty smell of fermentation that is so evocative; rich, sweet and savoury all at once.

PORK & VEGETABLE BIBIMBAP

Place the pork in a bowl. Combine all the marinade ingredients with 1 tablespoon cold water, add to the pork and stir well. Cover and marinate for at least 1 hour.

Cook the rice according to the packet instructions. Keep warm.

Heat the oil in a wok or frying pan/skillet over a medium–high heat. Add the pork slices and stir-fry for 2–3 minutes until evenly browned. Keep warm.

Heat 1 cm/½ in. vegetable oil in a small frying pan and fry the eggs for 2 minutes, or until the whites are cooked and the yolks are cooked but still runny.

Divide the rice between bowls and top each one with the prepared lettuce, carrot, cucumber, avocado and onion slices. Arrange the pork in the centre and top each bowl with a fried egg. Garnish with sesame seeds and serve with a bowl of kimchi on the side.

300 g/10½ oz. pork fillet, thinly sliced

200 g/7 oz. jasmine rice

2 tablespoons vegetable oil, plus extra for shallow frying

2 eggs

50 g/1¾ oz. iceberg lettuce, shredded

1 large carrot, peeled and grated

¼ cucumber, thinly sliced

½ avocado, sliced

½ small red onion, thinly sliced

sesame seeds, to garnish

kimchi, to serve

MARINADE

2 tablespoons gochujang

2 tablespoons caster/granulated sugar

2 garlic cloves, crushed

1 tablespoon dark soy sauce

½ tablespoon gochugaru

½ tablespoon toasted sesame oil

1 teaspoon sea salt

¼ teaspoon ground black pepper

Serves 2

This Malay version of Singapore crab was served to me on a trip to a small island named Mud Island. However, where there's mud there are mud crabs and this tiny island built on stilts, just off the west coast of Malaysia, is home to thousands of crabs and almost as many restaurants serving delicious platefuls of crab any which way.

CRAB & NOODLE STIR-FRY

Put the onion, garlic, ginger and chillies in a food processor and blend to a smooth paste. Stir in the shrimp paste and set aside for a moment.

Heat the oil in a wok or large frying pan/skillet set over a medium heat and fry the paste for 3–4 minutes until fragrant. Add the Shaoxing and simmer for 1 minute before stirring in the passata, stock, soy sauce and ketjap manis. Cook for 10 minutes until thickened.

Add the prepared crab and spring onions, stir well, cover and simmer for 5–8 minutes until the crab is cooked through.

Meanwhile, cook the noodles by plunging them into a large saucepan of boiling water. Return to the boil and cook for 4 minutes until al dente. Drain the noodles, shake well to remove excess water and divide between serving dishes.

Spoon the crab sauce over the top of each dish and serve sprinkled with extra spring onions.

TIP: It's best to use a live crab for this recipe, so ask your fishmonger to kill the crab for you and, if possible, to cut it up ready to stir-fry. Alternatively, view the process online to see how to do it yourself. If you don't feel confident doing this, use 1 kg/2 lb. cooked crab claws, cracking the shells with a hammer, and continue as above.

1 onion, roughly chopped

4 garlic cloves

2.5-cm/1-in. piece of fresh ginger, peeled and chopped

2 small red bird's eye chillies/chiles

1 tablespoon shrimp paste

3 tablespoons peanut oil

50 ml/scant ¼ cup Shaoxing rice wine

250 ml/1 cup tomato passata

250 ml/1 cup chicken stock

3 tablespoons light soy sauce

1 tablespoons ketjap manis

1 kg/2 lb. fresh crab, prepared (see Tip)

2 spring onions/scallions, finely chopped, plus extra to garnish

400 g/generous 3 cups fresh egg noodles (or 200 g/7 oz. dried egg noodles)

Serves 4

This recipe takes its name from the Japanese oversized bowl in which it is served. Fish, meats or vegetables are simmered together in a sauce and then served over rice in a donburi bowl.

DONBURI BEEF

Start by pickling the mushrooms. Place the dried mushrooms in a bowl and add plenty of boiling water to cover. Set aside for 20 minutes to soak. Drain the mushrooms and reserve 150 ml/⅔ cup of the liquid. Carefully slice off the mushroom stalks and discard.

Combine the mushrooms, reserved mushroom liquid, light soy sauce, vinegar, sugar and a pinch of salt in a small saucepan. Bring to the boil, stirring, and then simmer gently, partially covered, for 30 minutes. Remove from the heat and cool completely. Once cool, drain the liquid and thinly slice the mushrooms. Place the mushrooms in a jar and pour over the poaching liquid. Store for 1 week in the fridge; use as required.

Cook the rice according to the packet instructions. Keep warm.

Make the donburi sauce. Place all the ingredients in a bowl and stir to mix together well.

Transfer the sauce to a large frying pan/skillet and add the onion, garlic and ginger. Bring to the boil and simmer gently for 5 minutes until the onions are softened. Increase the heat to high, add the beef and cook for a further 5–10 minutes until the beef is browned and slightly sticky.

Divide the cooked rice between bowls, flattening slightly. Divide the beef and onion mixture between the bowls and add the pickled mushrooms and all the garnishes.

200 g/7 oz. Japanese medium-grain rice
1 onion, finely chopped
2 garlic cloves, thinly sliced
2-cm/1-in. piece of fresh ginger, peeled and shredded
600 g/1 lb. 5 oz. minced/ground beef

PICKLED MUSHROOMS
25 g/1 oz. dried shiitake mushrooms
60 ml/¼ cup light soy sauce
60 ml/¼ cup rice wine vinegar
30 g/2 tablespoons caster/granulated sugar
a pinch of salt

DONBURI SAUCE
200 ml/¾ cup dashi
50 ml/3½ tablespoons mirin
50 ml/3½ tablespoons dark soy sauce
1½ tablespoons honey

GARNISH
spring onions/scallions, thinly sliced
cucumber, thinly sliced
a handful of mixed salad leaves

Serves 4

This Malay version of pad Thai combines both Thai and Chinese elements and goes some way to portraying the blend of culinary cultures so typical of the country. This recipe serves two but can easily be doubled to serve up to four people.

FLAT NOODLE STIR-FRY
with prawn & Chinese sausage

Soak the noodles in a bowlful of hot water for 20–30 minutes until softened. Drain well, pat dry with a clean kitchen cloth and set aside in a mixing bowl.

To make the sauce, whisk all the ingredients together in a small mixing bowl. Set aside.

Heat the oil in a large wok or frying pan/skillet set over a medium–high heat and add the garlic and shallots, frying for 20 seconds. Add the prawns and sliced sausage and stir-fry for 2 minutes until the prawns change colour. Then add the beansprouts and sliced fish cake and stir-fry for 1 minute.

Stir in the noodles and sauce, and with a spatula push the noodles to one side to make a hole. Crack the egg into the middle and break the yolk to blend with the white. Spoon the noodles back over the egg and leave for about 15 seconds.

Add the sambal olek and garlic chives and continue to stir-fry until the egg is cooked and the chives start to wilt.

Spoon into bowls and serve garnished with spring onions, coriander and garlic chive flowers.

100 g/3½ oz. dried rice stick noodles
1½ tablespoons vegetable oil
2 garlic cloves, crushed
2 Asian shallots, thinly sliced
12 raw prawns/shrimp, peeled and deveined
1 Chinese dried sausage, sliced
75 g/1⅓ cups beansprouts, trimmed
200 g/7 oz. cooked fishcakes, sliced (either shop-bought or home-made, see page 97)
1 egg
1 tablespoon sambal olek
1 tablespoon chopped garlic chives

SAUCE
2 tablespoons light soy sauce
1 tablespoon fish sauce
1 teaspoon caster/granulated sugar
¼ teaspoon ground white pepper

TO SERVE
spring onions/scallions, thinly sliced
a bunch of fresh coriander/cilantro
garlic chive flowers

Serves 2

To the north of Laos lies the Yunnan region of China and many dishes have migrated over the border into Laos. Here Chinese egg noodles are used rather than the rice noodles that are more typical of Laotian dishes. Use any green leaves you like for this dish – anything goes.

CRISPY NOODLES with stir-fried greens

Cook the noodles by plunging them into a large saucepan of boiling water. Return to the boil and cook for 5 minutes until al dente. Drain well, refresh under cold water and shake dry. Set aside.

Stir all the sauce ingredients together in a small mixing bowl, adding 3 tablespoons cold water, and set aside.

Preheat half the vegetable oil in a wok set over a medium heat and add the noodles in one layer. Add the soy sauce and fry for about 2–3 minutes until starting to brown, then flip over and cook for a further 2–3 minutes until crispy. Remove the noodles from the pan and transfer to a warmed platter.

Add the remaining oil to the wok and fry the garlic and spring onions for 1 minute until softened. Add the mixed greens and stir-fry for 1–2 minutes until wilted. Stir in the sauce and cook for 1 minute.

Spoon the vegetables and sauce over the noodles and top with the herbs and sesame seeds. Serve at once.

200 g/7 oz. dried egg thread noodles

4 tablespoons vegetable oil

1 tablespoon soy sauce

2 garlic cloves, sliced

4 spring onions/scallions, thickly sliced

500 g/9 cups mixed greens, choose from pak choi/bok choy, choi sum, spinach or kale

a handful each of fresh basil and coriander/cilantro

1 tablespoon sesame seeds, toasted

SAUCE

2 tablespoons oyster sauce

1 tablespoon fermented soy bean paste

1 tablespoon dark soy sauce

2 teaspoons sesame oil

1 teaspoon grated palm sugar/ jaggery

Serves 4

A variation of a typical Chinese stir-fried rice dish, here it is made with pork and prawn, but it can in fact be made with all meats, seafood and vegetables. It is a super versatile rice dish. The eggs, rather than being fried as a topping, are beaten and cooked as a thin omelette. This is then rolled and sliced into omelette curls.

STIR-FRIED RICE with pork & prawn

Heat 1 tablespoon of the oil in a wok until it is hot. Pour in the beaten eggs and leave for 10 seconds for the base to set. Gently stir the mixture with a spatula, making sure it cooks evenly, for 1 minute until just set, forming a thin omelette. Remove from the pan and let cool. Roll the omelette up and cut into 1 cm/½ in. thick slices. Set aside.

Combine the hoisin sauce, soy sauce, vinegar and sesame oil in a small bowl.

Add the remaining oil to the wok and stir-fry the onion, ginger and garlic for 30 seconds. Add the pork and stir-fry for 1 minute, then add the prawns and sugar. Stir-fry for a further 2 minutes until the pork and prawns are golden.

Add the rice and stir well, then pour in the hoisin sauce mixture. Continue to stir-fry for a further 1–2 minutes until the rice is heated through. Stir through half the sliced spring onion garnish.

Divide between bowls and garnish with the remaining spring onions, the omelette curls and coriander leaves, and serve drizzled with chilli sauce.

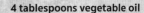

4 tablespoons vegetable oil

4 eggs, lightly beaten

3 tablespoons hoisin sauce

4 tablespoons light soy sauce

2 tablespoon rice wine vinegar

½ teaspoon sesame oil

1 small onion, thinly sliced

2 teaspoons grated fresh ginger

2 garlic cloves, thinly sliced

500 g/1 lb. 2 oz. pork fillet, thinly sliced

250 g/9 oz. small raw prawns/ shrimp, peeled and deveined

1 tablespoon caster/granulated sugar

800 g/1¾ lb. cooked long-grain rice, cooled and chilled

GARNISH

4 spring onions/scallions, sliced

fresh coriander/cilantro leaves

chilli/chili sauce

Serves 4

In Vietnamese cooking, the work is in the preparation, with very little time on the stove. My friends are always amazed that I can pull together a fried noodle dish when I haven't slaved all day in the kitchen. This recipe is a great way of using vegetables for a light meal. Adapt it with any kind of noodles and vegetables you have. You can add herbs like coriander/cilantro, garden mint or Thai sweet basil for something nutritious.

STIR-FRIED UDON NOODLES & Vegetables

Heat half the oil in a frying pan/skillet or wok and fry the onion until softened. Add the noodles, sugar, salt, pepper and soy sauce and fry, stirring quickly (with cooking chopsticks if you have them) for 5 minutes. Add a splash of the wine to steam the noodles, and keep separating them so that they don't stick together.

Transfer the mixture to a plate. In the same hot pan or wok, heat the rest of the oil, then fry the shallots until browned. Add the carrot, broccoli, mangetout and oyster sauce and stir-fry for 3 minutes. Add the beansprouts and remaining wine to help steam the vegetables, and cook for 2 minutes. Add the pak choi at the last minute.

Remove the pan from the heat, add the noodle mixture and stir well. Sprinkle with nuts and serve hot or at room temperature.

2 tablespoons cooking oil

½ red onion, sliced

400 g/14 oz. fresh udon noodles

a pinch of sugar

a pinch of salt

a pinch of ground black pepper

1 teaspoon light soy sauce

250 ml/1 cup white wine or water

2 Asian shallots or ½ red onion, diced

1 carrot, cut into matchsticks

4 stems of purple sprouting broccoli, roughly chopped

a small handful of mangetout/ snow peas, trimmed

1 tablespoon oyster sauce

40 g/½ cup beansprouts

1 head of pak choi/bok choy, roughly chopped

1 tablespoon crushed roasted salted peanuts or cashew nuts

Serves 2

FRESH & COOL

This tuna dish is just like sushi but in a bowl. The addition of plums adds an element of surprise, and brown rice brings an extra nuttiness, but otherwise the same but different!

CHIRASHI-ZUSHI

Cook the rice in a saucepan of boiling salted water according to the packet instructions until tender, then drain well and transfer to a bowl. Add the rice vinegar, maple syrup and ginger and stir the rice gently until thoroughly mixed. Set the rice aside for 15–20 minutes, stirring occasionally, until cool.

Meanwhile, for the sesame tuna, place a large non-stick frying pan/skillet over a medium–high heat. Rub the miso all over the tuna, then pat on the sesame seeds to cover. Place in the hot pan with the olive oil and sear for 1½ minutes on each side, so it is beautifully golden on the outside but blushing in the middle. Remove the tuna from the pan and slice, ready to serve.

Divide the rice between serving bowls, top with the seared tuna, radish, plum wedges, spring onions, avocado with the lime juice squeezed over, salmon roe, sesame oil to taste, sesame seeds, toasted nori, shiso and pickled ginger. Serve with wasabi and soy sauce on the side.

400 g/2 cups short-grain brown rice, rinsed
80 ml/⅓ cup rice vinegar
1 teaspoon maple syrup
a thumb-sized piece of fresh ginger, grated
400 g/14 oz. tuna (sushi grade)
1 tablespoon miso
3 tablespoons black sesame seeds
1 tablespoon olive oil

TO SERVE
4 radishes, julienned
1 plum, cut into thin wedges
4 spring onions/scallions, thinly sliced
1 avocado, thinly sliced
freshly squeezed juice of 1 lime
50 g/2 oz. salmon roe
a few drops of sesame oil
1 tablespoon toasted sesame seeds
toasted nori
shiso leaves
pickled ginger
wasabi
soy sauce

Serves 2

In marked contrast to other Asian cuisines, Japanese dishes are far simpler in their design and composition, with delicate flavours balanced perfectly. This dish of chilled noodles is traditionally served with three small cubes of ice in the middle to accentuate the cold. It would be eaten in the summer months only.

CHILLED SOBA NOODLES with dipping sauce

First, make the dashi broth. Pour 1.25 litres/quarts cold water into a saucepan, add the kombu and set aside for 30 minutes to soften. Bring the mixture to the boil over a medium heat, removing any scum that appears on the surface, then reduce the heat and simmer gently for 10 minutes. Remove from the heat, stir in the bonito flakes and allow the broth to cool. Strain and use immediately or chill for up to 3 days.

To make the dipping sauce. Whisk all the ingredients together in a bowl, or, if you have a clean glass jar with a lid, put all the ingredients into the jar, screw on the lid and shake well. Set aside in the fridge until needed.

Plunge the noodles into a large saucepan of boiling water and return to the boil. Cook for 4–5 minutes until the noodles are tender. Drain well and refresh under cold water, stirring until the noodles separate and the starch is removed. Drain again and leave to dry on a clean kitchen cloth until required.

For each serving, arrange a pile of spring onions, a little of the grated ginger, a little wasabi, a pinch of the dried nori and a bowl of the dipping sauce. Divide the noodles between small bowls and place 3 ice cubes in the middle of each one.

Serve with the garnishes and enjoy.

250 g/9 oz. dried soba noodles

2 spring onions/scallions, thinly sliced

2 teaspoons freshly grated ginger

2 teaspoons wasabi paste

5-cm/2-in. square of dried nori

12 ice cubes, to serve

DASHI BROTH

15 g/1 tablespoon chopped dried kombu

15 g/1 tablespoon dried bonito flakes

JAPANESE DIPPING SAUCE

200 ml/¾ cup dashi broth (see above)

3 tablespoons Japanese soy sauce

3 tablespoons mirin

½ teaspoon caster/granulated sugar

Serves 4

This summer salad can be made using any Japanese noodles. These black rice noodles make a startling contrast to the different vegetables and micro herbs when arranged on the plate giving a striking result.

CHICKEN NOODLE SALAD
with sesame and soy dressing

First, make the wafu dressing. Put all the ingredients in a sterilized glass jar, screw the lid on tightly and shake well until amalgamated.

Plunge the noodles into a large saucepan of boiling water. Return to the boil and simmer for 5–6 minutes until al dente. Drain the noodles and immediately refresh under cold water, washing well to remove any remaining starch. Drain again and dry thoroughly on a clean kitchen cloth. Put the noodles in a large mixing bowl and set aside.

Next, prepare the vegetables. Thinly slice the radishes, carrots and mangetout. Cut the cucumber into thin strips, like the carrot.

Arrange the noodles in the middle of each serving plate and place the vegetables in groups around them. Add the cooked chicken and drizzle over the dressing. Scatter over the micro herbs and sesame seeds and serve at once.

250 g/9 oz. dried black rice noodles

100 g/about 7 radishes, trimmed

2 carrots, trimmed

125 g/1½ cups mangetout/ snow peas, trimmed

½ cucumber, deseeded

250 g/1⅔ cups torn cooked chicken breast fillet

Japanese micro herbs

1 tablespoon black sesame seeds

WAFU DRESSING

1 small shallot, very finely chopped

2 tablespoons Japanese soy sauce

2 tablespoons rice wine vinegar

2 tablespoons dashi broth (see page 44)

2 teaspoons sesame oil

2 teaspoons caster/ granulated sugar

1 teaspoon freshly grated ginger

½ teaspoon crushed garlic

Serves 4

Traditionally bibimbap is a Korean hot rice dish but its versatility easily allows for it to be served as a salad, where the rice is cooked and cooled (see page 7) and then topped with a selection of vegetables, seared meats and a dressing. This dish is loosely based on a Thai seared beef salad, albeit with a Korean slant.

BIBIMBAP SALAD with seared beef

Start by making the marinade. Place all the ingredients in a bowl with 2 tablespoons cold water and stir well. Add the beef fillet and marinate for at least 1 hour, or overnight. Remove the beef from the marinade.

Make the dressing. Pound the seeds in a pestle and mortar or spice grinder to form a smooth paste. Gradually stir in the vinegar and remaining ingredients. Taste and adjust the amount of soy, sugar and vinegar to meet your required taste.

Heat a griddle or heavy-based frying pan/skillet over a high heat. Add the marinated beef and chargrill for 30–60 seconds on each side, depending on how rare you like your beef. Remove from the pan and set aside to rest for 5 minutes.

Divide the cooked rice between bowls and add the salad leaves, sliced cucumber, edamame, tomatoes and avocado. Slice the beef and divide between the bowls adding any juices. Drizzle over the sesame dressing and serve.

300 g/10½ oz. beef fillet steak

400 g/14 oz. cooked white long grain rice, cooled and chilled (see page 7)

2 handfuls of salad leaves or micro herbs

½ cucumber, thickly sliced

100 g/3½ oz. shelled edamame beans

50 g/1¾ oz. cherry tomatoes, halved

1 avocado, sliced

MARINADE

½ tablespoon gochujang

1 tablespoon sake

½ teaspoon gochugaru

1 tablespoon light soy sauce

½ tablespoon dark soy sauce

½ tablespoon soft brown sugar

SESAME DRESSING

3 tablespoons white sesame seeds

3 tablespoons white wine vinegar

3 tablespoons light soy sauce

3 tablespoons soft brown sugar

1 tablespoon sesame oil

Serves 2

Snaking its way through Vietnam, the Mekong Delta is home to the prawn/shrimp farming industry, producing large succulent prawns, perfect for grilling over coals on skewers as here.

CHAR-GRILLED PRAWNS
with noodle & herb salad

Peel the prawns, leaving the tail section intact. Cut down the back of each one and pull out the black intestinal tract. Wash and dry the prawns and put in a bowl with the soy sauce. Stir well and set aside to marinate for 30 minutes.

Meanwhile, make the nuoc cham. Put the chillies, garlic and palm sugar in a pestle and mortar or food processor and pound or blend to form a paste. Transfer to a mixing bowl and whisk in the remaining ingredients.

Thread each marinated prawn onto the soaked bamboo skewers from head to tail.

Soak the noodles in a bowlful of hot water for 20 minutes until softened. Drain and shake well to dry before transferring to a large mixing bowl. Toss the noodles with the sesame oil, then add the shredded papaya, salad leaves, herbs, micro herbs, spring onions, peanuts and deep-fried shallots.

Preheat a foil-lined stovetop grill pan over a high heat and cook the prawns for 2 minutes on each side until charred and cooked through.

Serve the prawns on the side of the salad bowls, drizzled with nuoc cham, garnished with shredded lime leaves and a squeeze of fresh lime.

TIP: Make a batch of crispy fried shallots to have on hand for all of your Asian rice and noodle bowls. Thinly slice about 12 shallots. Pour vegetable oil into a wok or (old) saucepan about 5 cm/2 in. up the side of the pan and set over a medium heat. Test the temperature of the pan by dropping a cube of bread into the hot oil – it should crisp within about 30 seconds. Deep-fry the shallots, in batches, for about 2–3 minutes, until crisp and golden. Remove with a slotted spoon and drain on paper towels. Serve immediately or store in an airtight container for up to 2 weeks.

24 large raw prawns/shrimp

1 tablespoon light soy sauce

150 g/5½ oz. rice vermicelli noodles

1 teaspoon sesame oil

½ green papaya, peeled and thinly sliced

50 g/1 cup mixed salad leaves

handful of fresh herbs such as mint and coriander/cilantro

small handful of mixed micro herbs

2–3 spring onions/scallions, trimmed and sliced

4 tablespoons peanuts, roasted and chopped

4 tablespoons deep-fried shallots (see Tip)

a few kaffir lime leaves, thinly sliced, to serve

lime wedges, to serve

NUOC CHAM

2 large red chillies/chiles, chopped

2 red bird's eye chillies/chiles, deseeded and chopped

2 garlic cloves, crushed

4 tablespoons grated palm sugar/ jaggery

4 tablespoons Thai fish sauce

grated zest and freshly squeezed juice of 4 limes

salt and pepper

24 bamboo skewers, soaked in cold water for 30 minutes

Serves 4

This salad celebrates freshness by combining a selection of (your) favourite crunchy veg and salad greens over rice with seeds and nuts for extra crunch. It is both fresh and satisfying, and the spice from the hit of wasabi is perfect.

CRISPY ASIAN RICE BOWL

Make the dressing. Place all the ingredients in a screw top jar, seal and shake well until amalgamated.

Divide the rice between bowls and top with the salad ingredients in separate groups. Top with the peanuts and drizzle over the salad dressing. Garnish with coriander and black sesame seeds.

400 g/14 oz. cooked long-grain brown rice

½ Nashi pear, cored and cut into matchsticks

50 g/1¾ oz. radishes, sliced

50 g/1¾ oz. sugar snaps, trimmed and shredded

50 g/1¾ oz. shelled edamame beans

50 g/1¾ oz. beansprouts

2 handfuls of salad leaves or pea shoots

25 g/1 oz. sprouted seeds, such as alfalfa

1 tablespoon salted peanuts, chopped

WASABI DRESSING

3 tablespoons soy sauce

3 tablespoons rice wine vinegar

2 tablespoons mirin

1 tablespoon caster/granulated sugar

2 teaspoons wasabi paste

GARNISH

fresh coriander/cilantro leaves

black sesame seeds

Serves 2

You can use any type of Japanese noodle for this, but I love the flavour and colour of green tea noodles. The deeply sweet flavour of green tea pairs wonderfully with the soft and soothing texture of the salmon.

SEARED SALMON & GREEN TEA NOODLE SALAD

Cook the noodles by plunging them into a large saucepan of boiling water. Return to the boil and cook for 4 minutes until al dente. Drain and immediately refresh under cold water before draining again. Shake to remove any excess water and dry with a clean cloth. Transfer the noodles to a large mixing bowl, add the sesame oil and toss well to coat.

Meanwhile season the salmon with the salt and mixed sesame seeds.

Preheat a non-stick frying pan/skillet over a high heat until smoking, add the salmon and cook for 1 minute on each side until seared on the outside but still rare inside. Set aside to cool before slicing thinly.

To make the dressing, combine all the ingredients in a bowl and stir to dissolve the sugar.

Arrange the noodles on a large platter and top with the salmon and coriander and salad leaves. Drizzle with the dressing and serve with some pickled ginger, if using.

TIP: Flavoured sea salts are all the rage and smoked sea salt is a lovely addition here. However, you can use regular sea salt if you prefer.

200 g/7 oz. green tea soba noodles

2 teaspoons sesame oil

250 g/9 oz. fresh sashimi salmon fillet

a pinch of smoked sea salt (see Tip)

3 tablespoons white and dark sesame seeds

a handful each of fresh coriander/cilantro and mixed baby salad leaves

pickled ginger, to serve (optional)

DRESSING

2 tablespoons dashi broth (see page 44)

1½ tablespoons rice wine vinegar

2 teaspoons light soy sauce

1 teaspoon caster/granulated sugar

1 teaspoon sesame oil

Serves 4

The black cloud ear fungus mushrooms used here add a delightful crunch to this Chinese-style tofu salad. You can use plain tofu if you prefer, but I love the slight smokiness from marinated tofu. Different flavours of tofu can be found in most large supermarkets or health food stores, so try out a few varieties to see which you like best.

EGG NOODLE, BLACK CLOUD EAR FUNGUS & TOFU SALAD

Put the black cloud ear fungus in a large mixing bowl, cover with boiling water and soak for 20 minutes until softened. Drain well, pat dry with paper towels and slice thinly, discarding any tough stalks. Set aside.

Meanwhile, cook the noodles by plunging them into a saucepan of boiling water. Return to the boil and simmer for 2–3 minutes until al dente. Drain and immediately refresh under cold water before draining again. Dry thoroughly using a clean kitchen cloth and set aside.

Cut the cucumber and carrot into thin strips and place in a large mixing bowl. Add the black cloud ear fungus, tofu, spring onions, cabbage and herbs and toss well.

To make the dressing, whisk all the ingredients together in a small bowl until the sugar is dissolved.

Stir the noodles into the salad, add the dressing and toss well until evenly combined. Serve in bowls, sprinkled with the sesame seeds.

15 g/1 cup dried black cloud ear fungus

200 g/7 oz. fresh egg noodles

½ cucumber, peeled

1 large carrot

150 g/1 cup marinated tofu, thinly sliced

4 spring onions/scallions, thinly sliced

100 g/1⅔ cups Chinese cabbage, sliced

a small handful each of fresh mint and coriander/cilantro

1 tablespoon sesame seeds, toasted

DRESSING

2 tablespoons light soy sauce

2 tablespoons brown rice vinegar

1 tablespoon caster/granulated sugar

1 teaspoon sesame oil

1 teaspoon chilli/chili oil

Serves 4

This is the kind of endgame of rice bowl salads. It is packed full of flavour, texture and nutritious ingredients, perfectly balanced with a sweet and savoury sesame dressing. It is the ideal summer salad, vibrant and joyful. I like to combine different coloured rice, but any kind works well.

JAPANESE SUPERBOWL RICE SALAD

Make the dressing. Combine the ingredients in a bowl and stir well. Leave to infuse for 30 minutes.

Cut the tuna into 1-cm/½-in. dice and place in a bowl. Add 1 tablespoon of the dressing, stir well and set aside while preparing the salad.

Divide the rice between bowls and add all the salad ingredients. Top with the tuna and drizzle over the remaining dressing.

TIP: To rehydrate seaweed simply place the dried flakes in a bowl and cover with plenty of cold water – watch and be awed as it quadruples in size as it soaks up the water.

150 g/5½ oz. fresh tuna (sushi grade)

400 g/14 oz. cooked red or black rice, cooled and chilled (see page 7)

100 g/3½ oz. silken tofu, drained and diced

50 g/1¾ oz. shelled edamame beans

50 g/1¾ oz. mangetout/snowpeas, trimmed, blanched and halved

¼ cucumber, thinly sliced

2 tablespoons wakame or dried seaweed mix, rehydrated (see Tip)

1 spring onion/scallion, thinly sliced

½ avocado, sliced

1 tablespoon pumpkin seeds

1 tablespoon black sesame seeds

a handful of salad leaves

SESAME & GINGER DRESSING

2 tablespoons sunflower oil

1 tablespoon sesame oil

4 tablespoons dark soy sauce

1 tablespoon rice wine vinegar

1 tablespoon clear honey

2 teaspoons grated root ginger

Serves 2

Green papaya salad is one of my favourite Asian dishes and, like many noodle dishes, varies in flavour enormously. But it is always hot, sour, salty and sweet. I love this version, which uses smoked pancetta for added saltiness and texture.

GREEN PAPAYA & CRISPY PORK SALAD

Soak the noodles in a bowlful of hot water for 10–20 minutes until softened. Drain well, pat dry with a kitchen cloth and set aside in a large mixing bowl.

Dry-fry the pancetta in a small frying pan/skillet set over a high heat until crisp and golden. Set aside to cool.

Thinly slice the papaya and cut into long thin strips or julienne. Add to the noodles with the cucumber, herbs, cherry tomatoes and pancetta.

Whisk together the fish sauce, sugar and lime juice and stir until the sugar is dissolved. Pour over the salad, toss well and divide the salad among plates.

Top with the fresh red chillies, if using, peanuts and powdered rice, and serve with deep-fried shallots.

NOTE: Used mainly in Thai cookery, toasted ground rice is made by toasting grains of rice in a wok and then grinding them in a pestle and mortar to form a powder. It is traditionally used in large salads and has a smoky, nutty flavour.

150 g/5 oz. dried rice vermicelli noodles

150 g/5 oz. pancetta, diced

150 g/⅓ green papaya, peeled, halved and deseeded

1 cucumber, deseeded and thinly sliced

a small bunch each of fresh Vietnamese mint, coriander/cilantro and Thai basil

125 g/scant 1 cup cherry/grape tomatoes, halved or quartered

2 tablespoons fish sauce

2 tablespoons grated palm sugar/jaggery

2 tablespoons freshly squeezed lime juice

2 red bird's eye chillies/chiles, deseeded and thinly sliced (optional)

4 tablespoons dry-roasted peanuts, finely chopped

1 tablespoon toasted ground rice (see Note)

deep-fried shallots, to serve (see page 51)

Serves 4

Simplicity at best. This is a salad packed with nourishing elements. It is definitely one of those dishes that you can make on a Sunday for your prep-ahead lunches. It travels well, and the dressing is all it needs for a toasty, savoury finish.

MISO BROWN RICE SALAD
with tofu & ginger dressing

Start by making the dressing. Mix all the ingredients together and set aside.

Preheat the oven to 200°C (400°F) Gas 6.

Wrap the tofu in paper towels or a kitchen towel and place on a baking sheet. Weigh down with something heavy, like a frying pan/skillet and let it sit for 10 minutes. Unpack and unwrap the tofu, then transfer to a cutting board and cut into 5-cm/2-in. cubes. Whisk together the ginger, soy sauce, white miso and honey. Add the tofu and gently toss to coat. Sprinkle the cornflour over and mix until incorporated. Let sit for 10 minutes.

Remove the tofu from the marinade and spread the cubes out on the lined baking sheet. Bake in the preheated oven for 25–30 minutes, turning halfway through, until golden brown and a thin crust forms.

Divide the rice between plates, then top with edamame, sliced radishes, beetroot and the tofu. Drizzle with the dressing and finish with coriander and dried chilli flakes.

250 g/generous 1¼ cups brown sushi rice, cooked according to packet instructions

200 g/7 oz. shelled edamame beans

100 g/3½ oz. radishes, sliced

2 golden beetroot/beets, grated

handful of fresh coriander/cilantro

pinch of dried chilli/hot red pepper flakes

DRESSING

thumb-sized piece of fresh ginger, grated

4 spring onions/scallions, thinly sliced

3 tablespoons white miso

1 garlic clove, crushed

1 tablespoon rice vinegar

2 tablespoons sesame oil

TOFU

300-g/10½-oz. pack tofu

thumb-sized piece of fresh ginger, grated

60 ml/¼ cup soy sauce

2 tablespoons white miso

2 tablespoons honey

1 tablespoon cornflour/cornstarch

baking sheet, lined

Serves 2

We all know just how yummy teriyaki is – a Japanese favourite with the rich flavours of dark soy, rice-flavoured sake, mellowed with sweet mirin. Although not typically served in a bowl, it does however lend itself well to this and provides a very satisfying bowl food meal.

TERIYAKI CHICKEN & stir-fried vegetables

Cook the rice according to packet instructions. Keep warm.

Make the teriyaki sauce. Combine the ingredients in a small saucepan and heat gently, stirring to dissolve the sugar. Set aside.

Make the dressing. Place all the ingredients in a bowl and stir well.

Heat the vegetable oil in a heavy-based frying pan/skillet over a high heat. Add the chicken and sear for 2 minutes on each side until golden. Lower the heat to medium, then add the teriyaki sauce. Cook for about 3–4 minutes until the chicken is cooked through and the sauce is sticky and thickened. Transfer the chicken to a board and let it cool for 5 minutes, then slice thickly. Reserve the pan and board juices.

Meanwhile, cook the broccoli, mangetout and asparagus for 1 minute until al dente. Drain and dry thoroughly. Add the dressing and stir well.

Divide the rice between bowls and top with the broccoli, mangetout and asparagus. Arrange the chicken slices on top and drizzle over the teriyaki sauce. Garnish with coriander leaves to serve.

400 g/14 oz. long-grain brown rice

2 tablespoons vegetable oil

700 g/1½ lb. skinless boneless chicken thighs

100 g/3½ oz. broccoli, cut into florets

100 g/3½ oz. mangetout/ snowpeas or sugar snaps, trimmed

100 g/3½ oz. asparagus spears, cut into lengths

fresh coriander/cilantro leaves, to garnish

TERIYAKI SAUCE

60 ml/¼ cup dark soy sauce

60 ml/¼ cup sake

2 tablespoons mirin

1 tablespoon caster/granulated sugar

CITRUS SOY DRESSING

1 tablespoon dark soy sauce

1 tablespoon sesame oil

½ tablespoon lemon juice

½ tablespoon maple syrup

Serves 4

SOUL SATISFYING

What distinguishes a Korean dolsot with bibimbap is actually the bowl in which it is served. A dolsot bowl is a stone (or earthenware) bowl that is preheated before the food is added to serve. It allows the rice at the bottom of the dish to crisp slightly, adding a bite of texture. Use any heatproof bowl you have.

BEEF DOLSOT BIBIMBAP

Place the beef in a bowl and add the apple juice, garlic, soy sauce and honey. Stir well and leave to marinate for at least 1 hour. Remove the beef from the marinade and dry well, reserving the marinade juices.

Cook the rice according to the packet instructions. Keep warm.

Preheat the oven to 220°C (425°F) Gas 7 for 10 minutes. Put two heat-proof serving bowls into the oven to get really hot.

Make the bibimbap sauce. Place all the ingredients in a bowl with 1 tablespoon cold water and stir well. Set aside.

Prepare the vegetables. Heat the sesame oil in a frying pan/skillet and stir-fry the garlic and spring onions for 2 minutes until softened. Stir in the sesame seeds and remove from the heat.

Blanch the spinach for 30 seconds in boiling water. Drain and squeeze dry. Place in a bowl and keep warm.

Heat the vegetable oil in a frying pan and stir-fry the carrot for 2 minutes until lightly golden. Transfer to a bowl. Repeat with the mushrooms for 2–3 minutes until softened. Transfer to a bowl. Divide the spring onion mixture equally between the vegetables, stir well and keep warm.

Cook the beef. Heat the vegetable oil in a heavy-based frying pan and, when hot, add the marinated beef. Stir-fry for 2 minutes until browned. Add the marinade juices, simmer and then remove from the heat.

Carefully remove the hot bowls from the oven and add 1 teaspoon of sesame oil to each one. Divide the rice between the bowls and press down with a spatula. Top each one with the beef, the vegetables and bibimbap sauce.

300 g/10½ oz. beef fillet, sliced thinly
60 ml/¼ cup apple juice
2 garlic cloves, crushed
2 tablespoons dark soy sauce
1 tablespoon clear honey
200 g/7 oz. Japanese rice
1 tablespoon vegetable oil
2 teaspoons sesame oil, plus extra to serve

BIBIMBAP SAUCE
4 tablespoons gochujang
2 tablespoons caster/granulated sugar
1 tablespoon light soy sauce
1 tablespoon sesame oil

VEGETABLES
1 tablespoon sesame oil
2 garlic cloves, finely chopped
2 spring onions/scallions, thinly sliced
1 tablespoon sesame seeds, toasted
60 g/2 oz. spinach leaves, stalks removed
1 tablespoon vegetable oil
1 carrot, cut into matchsticks
60 g/2 oz. shiitake, oyster or enoki mushrooms, sliced

Serves 2

It's no wonder chicken soup is known for its soothing medicinal properties, as well as its flavour – it tastes so good and so healthy with an underlying hint of ginger and garlic from the stock. This is a simple soup, but with a really good stock as a base it's hard to beat.

CHICKEN NOODLE SOUP

Plunge the noodles into a saucepan of boiling water and cook for 3–4 minutes until al dente. Drain, refresh under cold water and shake dry. Set aside.

Pour the stock into a large saucepan with the ginger, soy sauce, rice wine and oyster sauce and set over a medium heat. Bring slowly to the boil, then simmer for 5 minutes.

Stir in the chicken, pak choi and spring onions and simmer for 3–4 minutes until the chicken is cooked.

Divide the noodles between bowls, pour over the chicken soup and serve with some sliced chillies and fresh coriander, if using.

TIP: If using fresh Hokkein noodles, cook for 2 minutes instead of 3–4. If using vacuum-packed, pre-cooked noodles rinse under boiling water only before use. For either you will need 500 g/1 lb. 2 oz.

200 g/7 oz. dried Hokkein noodles
1.25 litres/quarts chicken stock
2 teaspoons freshly grated ginger
2 tablespoons light soy sauce
2 tablespoons Shaoxing rice wine
1 tablespoon oyster sauce
200 g/1½ cups sliced chicken breast fillet
250 g/about 6 whole pak choi/ bok choy, trimmed and roughly chopped
2 spring onions/scallions, thinly sliced, plus extra to serve
salt

GARNISHES (OPTIONAL)
fresh chillies/chiles, sliced
a small bunch of fresh coriander/ cilantro

Serves 4

This recipe is a great way of cooking a fish fillet, with the crisp garlic flakes adding both flavour and texture. Serve with rice and a green vegetable, such as spinach or pak choi/bok choy.

THAI-STYLE FISH with fried garlic

Preheat the oven to 200°C (400°F) Gas 6.

Remove the tough outer casing from the lemon grass. Finely chop the white, bulbous part, discarding the rest.

Place the fish, skin-side down, in a shallow ovenproof dish or roasting pan. Mix together 1 tablespoon of the oil, the fish sauce, shallot, chilli and lemongrass, season with pepper and pour evenly over the fish, coating it well. Bake the fish for 15–20 minutes until cooked through.

Just before the fish has finished cooking, heat the remaining oil in a small frying pan/skillet. Add the garlic and fry until golden-brown, taking care not to burn it, as this would make it bitter. Pour the hot garlic and oil over the cooked fish and serve at once.

1 lemon grass stalk
500 g/1 lb. 2 oz. white fish fillet (such as cod)
2 tablespoons sunflower or vegetable oil
1½ tablespoons fish sauce
1 shallot, finely chopped
1 red chilli/chili, deseeded and finely chopped
4 garlic cloves, thinly sliced lengthways
freshly ground black pepper

Serves 4

FRAGRANT BREAKFAST SOUP with rice

This is a flavoursome Thai-style vegetable and rice soup, traditionally eaten at breakfast, using leftover cooked rice.

Add all the stock ingredients to a large pan with 2 litres/quarts water and bring to the boil. Reduce to a simmer and cook for 10–15 minutes, then remove from the heat and leave to cool. Pour the stock through a sieve/strainer into a jug/pitcher, removing the stems and lemon grass.

Place the empty pan back over a medium heat. Add the oil and shallots and fry for 10–15 minutes until translucent. Set aside.

For the crispy garlic and onion, add the oil to a small frying pan/skillet. Add the garlic to the cool oil and then place over a medium–high heat. When the garlic starts to fry, stir well and reduce the heat to low. Keep stirring and frying gently until eventually the garlic starts to turn golden brown. Turn off the heat. Remove with a slotted spoon and drain on paper towels.

Place the same pan of oil back over a medium–high heat and then add the sliced onion (top up the oil if needed). Fry until the onion is deep golden brown and crispy. Remove with a slotted spoon and drain on paper towels. Set aside.

Add the strained stock and cooked rice to the shallot pan, and bring to a simmer (if using uncooked rice, cook over a medium heat for 10 minutes until about 75 per cent cooked). Add the chopped vegetables (except the kale), 1 tablespoon of the crispy garlic and simmer for another 7–8 minutes until the vegetables are just tender and the rice is fully cooked. Add the kale and stir well for another minute or so. Add a little more water if needed.

To serve, add some rice and vegetables to a deep bowl, top up with broth and sprinkle with crispy garlic and onions, coriander and spring onions. Serve with pickled chillies, if using, and lime wedges on the side.

1 tablespoon vegetable oil

2 banana shallots, finely chopped

240 g/2 cups cooked brown basmati rice, or use any leftover cooked rice

1 carrot, peeled and cut into 1-cm/½-in. cubes

5 chestnut/cremini mushrooms, cut into 1-cm/½-in. cubes

½ small turnip or swede, peeled and cut into 1-cm/½-in. cubes

1 celery stick, cut into 1-cm/½-in. cubes

2 stems purple sprouting broccoli, cut into small florets, no bigger than 2 cm/¾ in. (reserve stems for stock)

¼ cauliflower, cut into small florets, no bigger than 2 cm/¼ in. (reserve stems for stock)

a large handful of black kale (cavalo nero), or use any dark cabbage, roughly chopped

STOCK

vegetable stems from the trimmed broccoli and/or cauliflower

2 lemon grass stalks, crushed and chopped

1 tablespoon doenjang (Korean bean paste)

2–3 teaspoons vegetable stock powder/bouillon

CRISPY GARLIC & ONION

250 ml/1 cup vegetable oil, for frying, plus extra if needed

1 garlic bulb, cloves separated and finely chopped

1 small onion, thinly sliced

TO SERVE

handful of fresh coriander/cilantro

2–3 spring onions/scallions, thinly sliced at an angle

2–3 hot chillies/chilis, thinly sliced, in rice vinegar (optional)

lime wedges

Serves 4

Many Japanese dishes are inspired by Chinese cuisine, and this particular dish originates from Szechuan. It's a dish that goes particularly well with steamed rice – maybe that's why the Japanese love it so much! Szechuan spices can be very fiery to the point of numbing, so I've created a milder, but still fragrant version, using aubergine/eggplant instead of meat. It's just as soft, but much lighter... guilt-free seconds are a must!

SZECHUAN TOFU & AUBERGINE RICE BOWLS

Dice the tofu into small cubes, then wrap in two layers of paper towels to remove any excess water. Set aside.

Meanwhile, to make the mapo sauce, combine the sake, red miso, mirin, soy sauce, honey and Szechuan broad bean chilli paste in a small bowl. Stir together and set aside.

Heat the toasted sesame oil and vegetable oil in a medium frying pan/skillet over a medium heat. Fry the garlic, ginger and leek for 1 minute to infuse the flavour into the oil, then add the aubergine. Fry for 2 minutes until browned.

Add the mapo sauce and 80 ml/⅓ cup water to the pan with the vegetables, reduce the heat to low and simmer, uncovered, for about 3 minutes.

Add the tofu cubes gently, then pour the katakuriko (potato starch) or cornflour and water mixture around the rim of the pan. Bring to the boil for about 1 minute to thicken the mixture slightly, then remove from the heat.

Divide the cooked rice between serving bowls and add the mapo tofu. Garnish the dishes with sliced spring onion.

400 g/14 oz. silken tofu (soft tofu)
1 tablespoon toasted sesame oil
1 tablespoon vegetable oil
2 garlic cloves, chopped
thumb-sized piece of fresh ginger, peeled and finely chopped
½ leek, thinly sliced
1 aubergine/eggplant, diced into small cubes

MAPO SAUCE
2 tablespoons sake
2 tablespoons red miso
1 tablespoon mirin
1 tablespoon soy sauce
2 teaspoon runny honey
1 teaspoon Szechuan broad/fava bean chilli/chili paste
½ tablespoon katakuriko (potato starch) or cornflour/cornstarch mixed with ½ tbsp cold water
400 g/3 cups cooked white Japanese rice, to serve
1 spring onion/scallion, thinly sliced, to garnish

Serves 2

When on a stop-over in Singapore I often make a trip into the famous Glutton Bay area for a delicious bowl of noodles. To get the best dish check out the hawkers' stalls and go for the one with the longest queue.

SINGAPORE NOODLES

Begin by making the sauce. Combine all the ingredients in a small mixing bowl and set aside.

Next, combine the curry powder with 2 teaspoons water to make a paste. Set aside.

Cook the noodles by plunging them into a large saucepan of boiling water. Return to the boil and cook for 1 minute until al dente. Drain well and rinse under cold water to remove any excess starch. Set aside.

Put the sunflower oil in a wok or large frying pan/skillet set over a high heat and warm until smoking. Add the prawns and stir-fry for 2–3 minutes until lightly golden. Remove with a slotted spoon and set aside.

Fry the char sui in the same pan for 1 minute, remove and set aside. Cook the spring onions and pepper for 2 minutes, remove from the pan and set aside.

Reduce the heat, add the beaten eggs and cook in a single layer for 2 minutes. Remove from the pan, roll up and allow to cool before cutting into thin strips.

Add the peanut oil to the wok and stir-fry the garlic and ginger for 1 minute, then stir in the reserved curry paste. Add the noodles to the pan with the reserved sauce and toss over a high heat for 2 minutes until heated through. Stir through the prawns, char sui, spring onions, peppers, egg strips, beansprouts and chives for 1–2 minutes until hot.

Serve in bowls garnished with chive flowers and some sambal olek.

2 teaspoons curry powder

300 g/2½ cups fresh egg noodles

2 tablespoons sunflower oil

300 g/4½ cups (about 30) raw prawns/shrimp, peeled and deveined

75 g/3 oz. char sui, sliced

a bunch of spring onions/ scallions, sliced

1 red (bell) pepper, thinly sliced

2 eggs, beaten

2 tablespoons peanut oil

2 garlic cloves, sliced

2.5-cm/1-in. piece of fresh ginger, peeled and cut into shreds

100 g/1¾ cups beansprouts, trimmed

6 garlic chives, snipped

garlic chive flowers, to garnish

sambal olek, to serve

SAUCE

2 tablespoons light soy sauce

1 tablespoon caster/granulated sugar

1 teaspoon sesame oil

2 tablespoons oyster sauce

2 tablespoons rice wine vinegar

Serves 4

Teriyaki is so popular now – you don't even have to go to a Japanese restaurant to have it. Supermarkets and grocery stores sell ready-made bottles of the sweet, soy-based glaze that you can use to marinate your chicken. But nothing beats the taste of a homemade teriyaki sauce. It is very easy to make, I like to add lime for an extra fragrant twist.

CHICKEN TERIYAKI with lime on quinoa rice

In a small bowl, mix together the soy sauce, mirin, brown sugar, sake, lime juice and zest to make the teriyaki sauce, stirring until the sugar has dissolved. Set aside.

Add ½ tablespoon of the vegetable oil to a frying pan/skillet over a medium heat. Add the leeks and fry until lightly browned on each side. Remove them from the pan and set aside.

Place the chicken pieces in a bowl and lightly toss with the katakuriko (potato starch) or cornflour to coat evenly all over.

Add the remaining ½ tablespoon vegetable oil to the same frying pan/skillet and fry the chicken, skin-side down, for 2 minutes until browned. Remove the pan from the heat briefly and remove the excess chicken fat by tilting the pan to the side and carefully soaking up the fat with 1–2 paper towels (taking care not to actually touch the surface of the hot pan with your hand).

Turn the chicken pieces over and cook for 2 minutes on the other side.

Add the leeks back into the pan, then pour over the teriyaki sauce, stirring to coat the chicken and leeks evenly. Simmer for 4–5 minutes over a medium-high heat until the sauce has thickened.

Divide the cooked rice and quinoa between serving bowls, then add the teriyaki chicken. Sprinkle with toasted sesame seeds and serve with yuzu kosho chilli paste, if you want some extra heat.

1 tbsp vegetable oil

2 leeks, chopped into 2-cm/¾-in. lengths

500 g/1 lb. 2 oz. boneless skin-on chicken thigh fillets, diced into bite-sized pieces

4 tbsp katakuriko (potato starch) or cornflour/cornstarch

TERIYAKI SAUCE WITH LIME

3 tablespoons soy sauce

3 tablespoons mirin

1 tablespoons soft light brown sugar

1 tablespoon sake

1 tablespoon lime juice and grated zest from ½ lime

TO SERVE

800 g/6 cups cooked Japanese rice and quinoa, to serve

toasted white and black sesame seeds

yuzu kosho chilli/chili paste, to serve (optional)

Serves 4

HUE NOODLE SOUP with beef & pork

This amazing noodle soup originates from Huế (the city of temples, emperor's palaces and dynasties in central Vietnam) and is spicy, bold and invigorating.

For the stock and cooked meat, bring a very large saucepan of water to the boil with the salt. Add the meat and bones and boil for about 10 minutes until scum forms on the surface. Remove from the heat and discard the water.

Wash the pan, add 3 litres/quarts fresh water and bring to the boil. Add the rested meat and bring to a gentle simmer. Skim off any scum and fat from the surface with a spoon. Add the chicken stock.

Heat a stove-top griddle pan over a high heat (do not add oil). Char the onion and lemon grass stalks on both sides. Add to the broth with the sugar, mooli and salt. Simmer for at least 2 hours with the lid on. Check occasionally and skim off any scum and fat as needed.

After 2 hours, remove the beef from the pan and allow it to rest slightly, then slice it thinly and store it in a sealed container until serving. Add the shrimp paste, pork bouillon, stock cube, if using, and fish sauce to the broth. In another pan, heat the oil and fry the garlic, diced lemon grass and chilli powder. Add to the broth with the annatto powder and simmer.

For the contents, mix the spring onions, onion and coriander. Put a serving of vermicelli in a big, deep soup bowl. Put the cooked beef on top and sprinkle with the onion mixture, cha chiên and mint, if using. Bring the broth to boiling point and pour enough over the vermicelli to submerge them.

Serve with lime wedges for squeezing into the soup. Place the other garnishes on the side and add them to your hue as desired.

STOCK & COOKED MEAT

- 2 tablespoons salt
- 1 kg/2¼ lbs. rib of beef
- 500 g/1 lb. beef shin/ flank
- 600 g/1 lb. 5 oz. chopped, boneless oxtail
- 2 pig's trotters (optional)
- 2 litres/8 cups chicken stock
- 1 large onion, peeled and ends trimmed
- 8 lemon grass stalks – 6 bashed and 2 finely diced
- 40 g/1½ oz. rock sugar
- 1 mooli/daikon, peeled
- 1 tablespoon salt
- 1 tablespoon shrimp paste
- 1 tablespoon pork bouillon
- 1 bún bò hue stock cube (optional)
- 4 tablespoons fish sauce
- 3 tablespoons cooking oil
- ½ bulb of garlic, cloves separated, peeled and finely chopped
- ½ teaspoon chilli/chili powder
- ½ tablespoon annatto powder

CONTENTS

- 2 spring onion/scallions, thinly sliced
- ½ red onion, thinly sliced
- 8 sprigs of fresh coriander/ cilantro, roughly chopped (stalk on)
- 450 g/1 lb. thick rice vermicelli, cooked according to packet instructions, drained and rinsed with hot water
- cha chiên Vietnamese ham, thinly sliced
- leaves from 8 sprigs of hot mint (optional)

GARNISHES

- lime wedges
- Thai sweet basil
- sliced bird's eye chillies/chiles
- beansprouts
- banana blossom (optional)
- curly morning glory (optional)
- cockscomb mint (optional)
- shiso/perilla (optional)
- very large lidded saucepan
- muslin/cheesecloth and kitchen twine

Serves 6–8

Like all Japanese dishes, it is the contrast of textures and flavours that defines this dish. The soft slurp of noodles is balanced with the crisp tempura batter which, once submerged into the hot stock, becomes soft, gooey and comforting to eat.

RAMEN with tempura prawns

Peel the prawns, leaving the tail section intact and reserving the shells and head. Cut down the back of each one and pull out the black intestinal tract. Wash and dry the prawns and set aside. Put the shells and heads in a saucepan set over a medium heat and pour in the broth. Bring to the boil, cover and simmer for 30 minutes. Strain through a fine mesh sieve/strainer and return the stock to the pan. Add the soy sauce and mirin and set aside.

Plunge the noodles into a saucepan of boiling water and cook for about 4 minutes, or until al dente. Drain, refresh under cold water and shake dry. Set aside.

To make the tempura batter, put the egg yolk, iced water and both flours in a large mixing bowl. Very lightly beat the mixture together using a fork to make a slightly lumpy but thin batter.

Return the broth mixture to a simmer, add the mangetout and seaweed and simmer for 2 minutes. Add the noodles and cook for 1 minute to heat through.

Meanwhile, heat about 5 cm/2 in. of oil in a wok or old saucepan until a cube of bread dropped into the oil crisps and turns brown in 20–30 seconds. Dip the prawns into the tempura batter, shaking off any excess. Fry in batches for 2–3 minutes until crisp and golden. Carefully remove the cooked prawns and drain on paper towels. Add a little of the remaining tempura batter to the oil and cook until crisp. Drain this and put with the prawns.

Divide the noodles between warmed soup bowls, add the tofu and spring onions, then pour over the soup. Top each with two tempura prawns and sprinkle the crispy batter bits into the soup. Serve at once.

8 large raw prawns/shrimp

1.5 litres/quarts dashi broth (see page 44)

125 ml/½ cup Japanese soy sauce

75 ml/scant ⅓ cup mirin

250 g/9 oz. dried ramen noodles

125 g/2 handfuls mangetout/snow peas, trimmed and thinly sliced

2 tablespoons dried wakame seaweed

150 g/1 cup plus 1 tablespoon cubed firm tofu

2 large spring onions/scallions, thinly sliced

vegetable oil, for deep-frying

TEMPURA BATTER

1 egg yolk

250 ml/1 cup iced water

100 g/¾ cup plain/all-purpose flour

2 tablespoons potato (or rice) flour

Serves 4

This quick, light, refreshing, sweet and tangy soup can be eaten day or night. The base is simple enough to embrace any herbs and extras such as fried tofu, fishcakes and ham. My mother often made it when we were growing up; she said it reminded her of her home town by the seaside.

CRAB, TOMATO & OMELETTE SOUP

Put the dried shrimps in a bowl, cover with warm water and allow to soak for 10 minutes. Drain and pat dry.

Put the stock, shrimps and tomatoes in a large saucepan over a high heat and bring to the boil. Season with the lemon or lime juice, sugar, fish sauce and shrimp paste, then reduce to a medium heat.

Put the crabmeat, eggs, salt, pepper and sugar in a bowl and beat with a fork until well mixed.

Bring the broth back to a gentle boil. Create a whirlpool in the broth by stirring it around quickly, then pour the egg mixture into the middle. Stop stirring once all the mixture is in. It will rise to the top and form a floating omelette.

Meanwhile, put the oil in a frying pan/skillet and fry the shallots until golden.

When ready to serve, make sure the pan of broth is still boiling, then break up any large pieces of omelette and add the browned shallots.

Put the cooked rice vermicelli in bowls with the fishcakes and ham, if using, and pour the broth over the top. Serve the garnishes on the side.

4 tablespoons dried shrimps

2 litres/quarts chicken, vegetable or pork stock

4 tomatoes, quartered

freshly squeezed juice of 1/2 lemon or lime

2 tablespoons sugar, plus extra to taste

3 tablespoons fish sauce

1 teaspoon shrimp paste

240 g/8 1/2 oz. canned (lump) crabmeat, squeezed of excess moisture

4 eggs

pinch of salt

pinch of black pepper

1 teaspoon cooking oil

2 Asian shallots, thinly sliced

TO SERVE

cooked rice vermicelli

1 quantity cooked Fishcakes, sliced (see page 97, optional)

cha chiên Vietnamese ham, thinly sliced (optional)

GARNISHES (OPTIONAL)

lime wedges

sliced bird's eye chillies/chiles

garden mint

hot mint

cockscomb mint

shiso/perilla leaves

Thai sweet basil

fresh coriander/ cilantro

banana blossom

curly morning glory

beansprouts

Serves 4

The name 'Hokkein noodles' refers both to a type of noodle and a noodle dish. Originally from the Hokkein province in China, the noodles and the dish spread in popularity to Malaysia and Singapore, and today are synonymous with stir-fried noodles around the world.

HOKKEIN NOODLES

Whisk together the ginger, Shaoxing, soy sauce and sesame oil in a shallow dish. Add the pork slices, toss well and set aside to marinate for 30 minutes. Remove the pork from the marinade and reserve both.

Meanwhile, cook the noodles by plunging them into a large saucepan of boiling water. Return to the boil and cook for 1–2 minutes until al dente. Drain, immediately refresh under cold water, drain again and dry well with a clean kitchen cloth. Set aside.

Put 2 tablespoons of the peanut oil in a wok and set over a medium heat until it starts to shimmer. Add the marinated pork and stir-fry for 2–3 minutes until lightly golden. Remove with a slotted spoon and set aside.

Heat the remaining oil in the wok and fry the carrots for 1 minute, add the pepper and garlic and fry for a further minute. Then stir in the mushrooms and fry for a further 2 minutes. Add the noodles and stir-fry for 1 minute.

Add the cooked pork, reserved marinade, oyster sauce, ketjap manis, 2 tablespoons water and the spring onions, and stir-fry until the noodles are hot.

Divide among bowls and serve garnished with spring onions.

2 teaspoons freshly grated ginger

3 tablespoons Shaoxing rice wine

3 tablespoons light soy sauce

2 teaspoons sesame oil

300 g/1½ cups sliced pork fillet

500 g/4 cups fresh Hokkein noodles (or 250 g/9 oz. dried)

4 tablespoons peanut oil

2 carrots, sliced

1 red (bell) pepper, sliced

4 garlic cloves, sliced

150 g/2½ cups shiitake mushrooms, thinly sliced

2 tablespoons oyster sauce

2 tablespoons ketjap manis

4 spring onions/scallions, sliced, plus extra, thinly sliced to garnish

Serves 4

A light, clean and refreshing bowl of goodness, this is the loveliest combination of prawns/shrimp, sugar snap peas and tofu – so nourishing for the mind and body. However, it can easily become a vegetable-based dashi broth by adding extra greens and omitting the prawns.

DASHI RICE GREEN TEA BROTH BOWL

Whisk the dashi and boiling water in a large saucepan over a high heat, add the rice and soy sauce and bring to the boil. Reduce the heat to medium-high and cook for 15–20 minutes until the rice is just tender.

Add the green tea bags, prawns, greens, sugar snap peas and ginger, remove the pan from the heat, and stir in the cubed tofu just to gently heat. Let stand for 3–4 minutes until the prawns are cooked through and the greens wilted.

Ladle the soup into warm bowls, discarding the green tea bags. Scatter with watercress sprigs and serve hot.

2 sachets instant dashi

2 litres/quarts boiling water

220 g/scant 1¼ cups sushi rice, rinsed under cold running water

60 ml/¼ cup soy sauce, plus extra to taste

2–3 green tea bags

16 raw prawns/shrimp, peeled and deveined

200 g/7 oz. mixed Asian greens

20 g/¾ oz. sugar snap peas, trimmed

a thumb-sized piece of fresh ginger, grated

200 g/7 oz. tofu, cut into cubes

a little watercress, to garnish

Serves 4

The Japanese word butadon actually translates as 'pork bowl' and refers to a dish of rice cooked with pork that has been simmered in a sweet, almost caramel sauce. It is served, simply, with pickles as this is all it requires. It is divine.

PORK BUTADON

Cook the rice according to the packet instructions. Keep warm.

Make the sauce. Place the sugar and 2 tablespoons cold water in a heavy-based saucepan and stir gently over a medium heat until the sugar dissolves. Stop stirring and bring the liquid to the boil. Cook for 2–3 minutes until the syrup turns a golden brown. Carefully (the liquid will spit) pour in the boiling water, then stir in the soy and sake. Bring to a simmer, cook for 1 minute, then remove from the heat. Set aside.

Heat the oil in a large frying pan/skillet over a high heat. Add the pork fillet slices and fry in batches for 1–2 minutes until browned. Once all are cooked, return them to the pan. Add the sauce to the pan and cook for a further 2 minutes until the pork is cooked through.

Meanwhile, cook the broccoli in a saucepan of lightly salted boiling water for 2 minutes. Drain.

Divide the rice between bowls and arrange the pork, broccoli and sauce over the top. Garnish with the pickled ginger, sliced spring onions and sesame seeds.

400 g/2¼ cups medium-grain rice
3 tablespoons vegetable oil
700 g/1 lb. 9 oz. pork fillet, thinly sliced
250 g/9 oz. Tenderstem broccoli or choy sum

CARAMEL SOY SAUCE
6 tablespoons caster/granulated sugar
120 ml/½ cup boiling water
90 ml/⅓ cup dark soy sauce
60 ml/¼ cup sake
2–3 teaspoons salt

GARNISHES
pickled ginger
spring onions/scallions, thinly sliced
black sesame seeds

Serves 4

This is sort of like crispy fish fingers on rice but a whole load more interesting. Fingers of white fish are coated in breadcrumbs and deep-fried to golden perfection. They are served on a bed of perfectly cooked rice and drizzled with a combination of barbecue sauce and Japanese mayonnaise. It is finger-licking good.

JAPANESE SAKANA FRY DON

Make the pickles. Place the carrot and mooli in a bowl and add 500 ml/2 cups cold water to cover. Stir in the salt and set aside for 10 minutes. Drain well and spoon the vegetables into a sterilized jar. Combine the boiling water and sugar and stir until dissolved. Add the vinegar and then pour the brine into the jar to cover the vegetables. Seal the jar. Store for up to 1 week in the fridge. Use as required.

Make the BBQ sauce. Place all the ingredients in a saucepan and bring to the boil. Simmer for 20 minutes until the liquid is reduced and slightly sticky. Strain through a fine sieve and allow to cool completely.

Cook the rice according to the packet instructions. Keep warm.

Cut the fish into goujons or shortish fish fingers. Season with salt. Dip into the flour, then the eggs and finally into the panko crumbs until completely coated. Place on a plate.

Heat 5 cm/2 in. vegetable oil in a wok or heavy-based saucepan until it reaches 180°C/350°F on a sugar thermometer. Add the fish pieces, a few at a time, and deep fry for 3–4 minutes until golden. Drain on kitchen paper and keep warm while cooking the remaining fish.

Divide the rice among bowls and top each one with the fried fish. Drizzle over a little BBQ sauce and a few pickles. Garnish with edamame beans, black sesame seeds and a drizzle of mayonnaise.

TIP: if you don't have a sugar thermometer to test the oil temperature add a cube of bread to the hot oil. It should immediately sizzle and brown the bread in 20 seconds.

400 g/14 oz. jasmine rice
750 g/1 lb. 10 oz. skinless
  white fish fillets
a pinch salt
30 g/2 tablespoons plain/
  all-purpose flour
2 eggs, beaten
100 g/3½ oz. panko crumbs
vegetable oil, for deep-frying
shelled edamame beans, black
  sesame seeds and Japanese
  mayonnaise, to serve

EASY PICKLES
1 carrot, shredded
200 g/7 oz. mooli/daikon,
  peeled and shredded
½ tablespoon salt
125 ml/½ cup boiling water
3½ tablespoons white sugar
180 ml/¾ cup white vinegar

BBQ SAUCE
1 small onion, finely chopped
1 large garlic clove, crushed
2½ tablespoons dark soy sauce
3½ tablespoons white sugar
100 ml/scant ½ cup pear
  or apple juice
½ tablespoon sesame oil
½ teaspoon salt
a pinch of black pepper

Serves 4

In this Vietnamese recipe, the broth is flavoured by fishcakes and fried shallots. This is a very versatile soup, so the broth can be made from any stock, and you can use fish fillets, seafood or meat such as chicken and pork.

UDON NOODLE SOUP with fishcakes

First, make the fishcakes. Put all the ingredients in a food processor and process until fine and well combined. Transfer the mixture to a bowl, cover and allow to rest for 1–2 hours or overnight – in which case, put it in the refrigerator.

When ready to cook, take two-thirds of the uncooked fishcake mixture and shape into a patty. Heat 1 tablespoon of the oil in a frying pan/skillet and fry the patty on both sides until golden. Cut into thin slices.

Pinch off bite-size pieces from the remaining uncooked fishcake mixture and roll into rough balls. Set aside.

Put the stock, pepper, sugar, salt, pork bouillon and fish sauce in a saucepan over a medium heat and bring to a gentle boil.

Meanwhile, heat the remaining oil in a frying pan/skillet and fry the shallots until brown and crispy.

Bring another pan of water to the boil and blanch the noodles for 2 minutes. Drain and divide them among soup bowls. Add the slices of fried fishcake and a generous pinch of the chopped herbs from the garnishes. Add more pepper to taste.

When ready to serve, make sure the pan of broth is still boiling, then add the uncooked fish balls. After a couple of minutes when they have floated to the surface, tip in the fried shallots. Ladle the soup into the prepared soup bowls.

Scatter over the remaining herbs to garnish, the deep-fried shallots and sliced chillies, and serve with lime wedges for squeezing.

3 tablespoons cooking oil

2 litres/quarts chicken, pork or vegetable stock

1/2 teaspoon coarsely ground black pepper

2 teaspoons sugar

2 teaspoons salt

1 teaspoon pork bouillon or 1 chicken stock cube (optional)

2 tablespoons fish sauce

8 Asian shallots, chopped

800 g/1¾ lbs. fresh udon noodles

FISHCAKES

300 g/10½ oz. skinless haddock or monkfish fillets, chopped

1 Asian shallot, chopped

1 bird's eye chilli/chile

1½ teaspoons sugar

1 teaspoon baking powder

a pinch of black pepper

2 tablespoons cooking oil, plus extra for oiling and frying

2 tablespoons fish sauce

1 tablespoon tapioca starch

a handful of fresh dill

GARNISHES

deep-fried shallots (see page 51)

fresh mint and coriander/cilantro, coarsely chopped

dill, finely chopped (optional)

sliced bird's eye chillies/chiles

lime wedges

Serves 4

WARMING SPICE

Laksa is a spicy noodle soup made with coconut milk and either seafood, pork or chicken. It is always adorned with a selection of garnishes. Malaysian food draws on its rich heritage of cultures from Chinese to Indian and these combine here with the use of spices, herbs and coconut to create a truly unique soup.

CHICKEN LAKSA

Soak the noodles in a bowlful of hot water for about 20–30 minutes until softened. Drain well, shake dry and set aside.

Put the chicken breast in a saucepan with the stock set over a low–medium heat. Simmer very gently for 10 minutes until the chicken is just cooked. Remove the chicken from the stock and set aside to cool completely. Once cool, slice thinly.

To make the laksa paste, pound all the ingredients together in a large pestle and mortar or blitz in a food processor until smooth.

Heat the oil in a wok or non-stick saucepan set over a medium heat and add the laksa paste. Fry for 2 minutes until fragrant, then add the coconut milk and chicken stock. Simmer gently for 10 minutes and then stir in the coconut cream, fish sauce and sugar. Simmer gently for a further 2–3 minutes.

Divide the noodles among bowls and add the sliced chicken. Pour over the hot soup and serve topped with a selection of garnishes. Pass around a pot of sambal olek or chilli oil, to drizzle.

250 g/9 oz. dried rice stick noodles

2 large skinless chicken breast fillets (about 350 g/12 oz.)

1 litre/quart chicken stock

2 tablespoons vegetable oil

400 ml/1²/₃ cups coconut milk

200 ml/³/₄ cup coconut cream

2 tablespoons fish sauce

2 teaspoons caster/granulated sugar

LAKSA PASTE

6 shallots, chopped

4 garlic cloves, chopped

2 lemon grass stalks, thinly sliced

2 large red bird's eye chillies/chiles, deseeded and sliced

2.5-cm/1-in. piece of fresh galangal, peeled and chopped

2.5-cm/1-in. piece of fresh turmeric, peeled and chopped (or 1 teaspoon ground turmeric)

4 macadamia nuts

1 tablespoon shrimp paste

2 teaspoons coriander seeds, toasted and ground

GARNISHES

beansprouts, trimmed

¹/₂ cucumber, sliced

deep-fried puffed tofu

deep-fried shallots (see page 51)

fresh coriander/cilantro or Vietnamese mint

1 lime, cut into wedges

sambal olek or chilli oil

Serves 4

Barbecuing is highly prized in Korean cooking and there are a host of different barbecued classics. Here beef short ribs are slow-cooked for several hours to render them tender. If you prefer to use a different cut of beef, you could use brisket or chuck steak. You will need to begin this recipe a day ahead.

SPICY BBQ KOREAN BEEF RICE BOWL

Combine the marinade ingredients in a bowl. Add the beef ribs, coat well and marinate overnight.

The next day, heat the oven to 150°C (300°F) Gas 2. Line a roasting pan with baking paper and lay the ribs on top. Cover the whole tin with foil and bake for 3 hours, or until the meat is falling from the bone. Don't be tempted to remove the beef from the oven until it is really tender.

Make the chogochujang sauce. Dry fry the sesame seeds in a small frying pan/skillet until evenly toasted. Transfer to a pestle and mortar (or spice grinder) and pound to a rough paste. Place in a bowl and stir in the gochujang, vinegar, soy sauce, honey and sesame oil until smooth, then add the spring onion and garlic and stir well. Set aside.

Cook the rice according to packet instructions. Keep warm.

Once the beef is tender. Heat a barbecue until hot or alternatively use a conventional grill/broiler heated to its highest setting. Cook the ribs for 10 minutes until really charred all over.

Arrange the rice in bowls. Top with the beef and all the garnishes. Serve with the sauce to drizzle or dip.

1 kg/2 lb. beef short ribs
400 g/2¼ cups Korean or
   Japanese sticky rice

MARINADE
3 garlic cloves
3 tablespoons soft brown sugar
4 tablespoons dark soy sauce
2 tablespoons sesame oil
1 tablespoon chilli/chili sauce
1 tablespoon freshly grated
   root ginger
2 star anise, lightly bashed

CHOGOCHUJANG SAUCE
1 tablespoon sesame seeds
1–2 teaspoons gochujang
2 tablespoons rice wine vinegar
2 tablespoons dark soy sauce
1 tablespoons clear honey
2 teaspoons sesame oil
1 spring onion/scallion,
   finely chopped
1 garlic clove, crushed

GARNISHES
carrots, shredded
avocado, thinly sliced
bean sprouts, trimmed
red onions, thinly sliced
cucumber, shredded
perilla leaves

Serves 4

This Vietnamese-inspired rice bowl encompasses the five flavours and elements of Vietnamese cuisine: sweet, sour, bitter, spicy and salty, all coming together for a taste sensation in one bowl.

VIETNAMESE-STYLE RICE BOWL
with chicken skewers & nuoc cham

For the chicken skewers, whisk together everything except the chicken together in a small bowl for 1 minute until combined and the sugar is starting to dissolve. Add the chicken chunks and stir to coat. Refrigerate overnight or for at least 4 hours. Meanwhile, soak the wooden skewers in water for at least an hour. Fire up the grill/broiler and allow it to become hot and fiery. Add a few chunks of chicken to each skewer and grill/broil until the chicken is cooked through and there's a nice char on the nuggets. Remove from the heat and set aside.

To make the nuoc cham, add 3 tablespoons water and the palm sugar to a bowl and stir for 1 minute until dissolved. Add in the lime juice, fish sauce, garlic and bird's eye chillies.

To cook the rice, heat the rapeseed oil in a saucepan, add the onion and cook to soften for a few minutes, then add the rice and turmeric and cook for a further minute. Add the ginger, lemon grass and 500 ml/2 cups water, bring to a simmer and cook, covered, for about 15 minutes. Turn off the heat. In a separate bowl dissolve the palm sugar in the fish sauce and lime juice and pour into the rice, fluffing it up with a fork. Keep covered until ready to serve.

To serve, divide the rice between bowls, top with the chicken skewers and add the mint, coriander, carrot, cucumber, lettuce, peanuts, lime wedges, nuoc cham and some sriracha for some extra kick.

CHICKEN SKEWERS
½ onion, finely chopped
3 garlic cloves, crushed
30 g/1 oz. palm sugar/jaggery
2 tablespoons soy sauce
1 tablespoon fish sauce
2 tablespoons sesame oil
500 g/1 lb. 2 oz. chicken breasts, cut into chunks

NUOC CHAM
2 tablespoons palm sugar/jaggery
freshly squeezed juice of 1 lime
2 tablespoons fish sauce
1 garlic clove, crushed
1–2 bird's eye chillies/chiles, chopped

RICE
1 tablespoon rapeseed/canola oil
½ onion, finely chopped
250 g/1⅓ cups jasmine rice

½ teaspoon ground turmeric
thumb-sized piece of fresh ginger, grated
1 lemon grass stalk, bruised
1 tablespoon palm sugar/jaggery
2 tablespoons fish sauce
freshly squeezed juice of 1 lime

TO SERVE
30 g/1 oz. fresh mint, leaves picked
30 g/1 oz. fresh coriander/cilantro, leaves picked
1 carrot, julienned
1 cucumber, julienned
2 Little Gem/Bibb lettuces, leaves separated
2 tablespoons peanuts, toasted
2 limes, cut into wedges
sriracha
8 long wooden skewers

Serves 2

There is something very appealing about bowl food. Here, classic Korean flavourings – including gochujang (Korean chilli paste), aromatic root ginger and pungent garlic – transform delicate, fresh exotic mushrooms into a piquant, flavourful topping for a bowl of rice.

GOCHUJANG-GLAZED MUSHROOM & WHOLE GRAIN RICE BOWLS

Place the rice in a heavy-based saucepan. Add 400 ml/1⅔ cups water and season with a pinch of salt. Bring to the boil, then reduce the heat, cover and simmer over a low heat for 25 minutes until the rice is tender.

About 5 minutes before the rice is ready, mix together the gochujang, rice wine, soy sauce and sugar in a small bowl to form a paste.

Heat the oil in a wok or large frying pan/skillet over a medium–high heat. Add the garlic, ginger and spring onions. Fry, stirring, for about 1 minute until fragrant. Add the red pepper, mushrooms, mangetout and cashews and stir-fry over a high heat for 2–3 minutes until the mushrooms are lightly browned. Add the gochujang paste mixture and stir in well to coat the ingredients. Stir-fry for 1–2 minutes until all the vegetables and mushrooms are glazed and sticky.

Divide the cooked and drained rice among bowls and top each portion with some of the glazed mushrooms and veg. Garnish with coriander and serve at once.

300 g/1½ cups whole grain brown rice, rinsed

2 teaspoons gochujang or sweet chilli sauce

2 tablespoons rice wine or Amontillado sherry

2 tablespoons light soy sauce

2 teaspoons sugar (just 1 teaspoon if using sweet chilli sauce)

1 tablespoon vegetable oil

1 garlic clove, chopped

thumb-sized piece of fresh ginger, chopped into fine strips

2 spring onions/scallions, white parts only, cut into short lengths

½ red (bell) pepper, cut into strips

400 g/14 oz. assorted fresh oyster, shiitake, king oyster or shiroshimeji mushrooms, any large ones sliced

50 g/⅔ cup mangetout/snowpeas, cut into short pieces

2 tablespoons raw cashew nuts

salt and freshly ground black pepper

handful of fresh coriander/cilantro sprigs, to garnish

Serves 4

This richly flavoured soup is hot and spicy so feel free to temper the heat to your tastes and perhaps bear in mind that most traditional recipes ask for four or five times the amount of spice than I use. I like to serve it with extra gochujang (Korean chilli sauce) on the side for guests to alter the heat of the broth themselves.

SPICY NOODLE SEAFOOD BROTH

Plunge the noodles into a saucepan of boiling water and cook for about 4 minutes or until al dente. Drain, refresh under cold water and shake dry. Set aside.

Heat the oil in a wok or large frying pan/skillet set over a high heat and stir-fry the ginger for 10 seconds. Add the pork and stir-fry for 2–3 minutes until browned. Add the spring onions, gochujang and soy sauce and fry for a further 2–3 minutes.

Add the vegetables, stir well, then stir in the stock. Simmer gently for 10 minutes until the vegetables are al dente.

Meanwhile, prepare the seafood. Wash and dry the clams, shell and devein the prawns/shrimp and cut along one side of the squid bodies to open out, insides up. Using a sharp knife, score a diamond pattern over the squid and cut into large pieces.

Add the seafood to the pan and cook gently until the clams have opened and the prawns and squid are cooked.

Add the noodles to warm through and serve at once.

200 g/7 oz. dried udon noodles

2 tablespoons vegetable oil

2.5-cm/1-in. piece of fresh ginger, peeled and thinly sliced

150 g/1 cup sliced pork fillet

2 spring onions/scallions, cut into batons

2–3 teaspoons gochujang, plus extra to serve

3 tablespoons dark soy sauce

1 large carrot, cut into batons

1 courgette/zucchini, cut into batons

100 g/1¾ cups sliced white cabbage

100 g/2 cups shiitake mushrooms, stalks trimmed and halved

1.5 litres/quarts chicken stock

24 small clams

20 raw prawns/shrimp

200 g/7 oz. cleaned squid bodies

Serves 4

As the name suggests, this dish originates from Chiang Mai in the north of Thailand. It can be served as a soup or a stew-like dish of noodles with a curried coconut sauce.

CHIANG MAI NOODLE CURRY

Put the shallots, garlic, turmeric and salt in a pestle and mortar and pound until fairly smooth. Stir in the red curry paste.

Add the coconut cream to a wok set over a medium heat and cook for about 3 minutes until the cream bubbles and splits. Stir in the curry paste mixture and continue to cook for a further 2 minutes. Stir in the palm sugar, fish sauce and soy sauce and bring to the boil. Add the chicken stock and lime leaves and simmer gently for 15 minutes.

Meanwhile, pour vegetable oil into a wok or large saucepan to reach about 5 cm/2 in. up the side of the pan and set over a medium heat. Test the temperature of the pan by dropping a cube of bread into the hot oil – it should crisp within 30 seconds. Carefully add 50 g/ 2 oz. of the noodles and deep-fry (be careful as the oil will spit) until crisp. Drain on paper towels and set aside to garnish.

Cook the remaining noodles by plunging them into a large saucepan of boiling water. Return to the boil and cook for 2–3 minutes until al dente. Drain well and divide among warmed bowls.

Stir the beef and coriander into the wok with the curry mixture and immediately remove the pan from the heat.

Spoon the curried beef and sauce over the noodles and serve with the deep-fried noodles, spring onions, deep-fried shallots and lime wedges.

2 red Asian shallots, chopped

1 garlic clove, roughly chopped

1-cm/½-in. piece fresh turmeric (or ½ teaspoon ground)

a pinch of salt

1 tablespoon Thai red curry paste

100 ml/⅓ cup coconut cream

2 tablespoons grated palm sugar/jaggery

1 tablespoon fish sauce

2 teaspoons dark soy sauce

600 ml/2½ cups chicken stock

4 kaffir lime leaves, pounded

500 g/1 lb. 2 oz. fresh egg noodles

250 g/1 cup thinly sliced beef fillet

2 tablespoons chopped fresh coriander/ cilantro

vegetable oil, for deep frying

TO SERVE

spring onions/scallions, shredded

deep-fried shallots (see page 51)

lime wedges

Serves 4

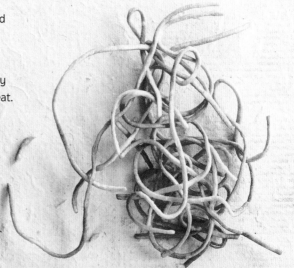

Asian Larb is a meat salad popular throughout Thailand and Laos in particular. It is always made with minced meat, which can be chicken, pork or beef. Although not traditional, the meat sits well on a bed of rice and the flavours from the sauce result in that distinctive delightful bite of hot, sweet, sour and savoury all at once.

VIETNAMESE BEEF LARB

Cook the rice according to the packet instructions. Keep warm.

Make the garlic paste. Heat a dry frying pan/skillet and, when hot, add the garlic cloves. Allow to brown all over for about 5 minutes. Cool and then remove the skins. Place the garlic in a pestle and mortar (or blender) with a little of the salt and pound together to form a paste. Add the lemon grass, ginger and chilli and pound all together to form a paste. Add the sesame seeds and remaining salt and pound again until smooth. Set aside.

Make the dressing. Place the chillies, garlic and palm sugar in a pestle and mortar (or blender) and pound to form a paste. Transfer to a bowl and whisk in the remaining ingredients.

Heat the oil in a wok or large frying pan and fry the garlic paste for 1 minute until fragrant. Add the beef and continue to stir-fry for 3–4 minutes until the beef is browned. Add the fish sauce and sugar and cook for a further 1 minute.

Divide the rice between bowls. Top with the beef mixture, carrot and fresh herbs. Drizzle over the dressing. Add the lettuce leaves and serve with crispy shallots.

400 g/2¼ cups jasmine rice

1 tablespoon peanut or vegetable oil

600 g/1 lb. 5 oz. minced/ground beef

2 tablespoons fish sauce

2 teaspoons white sugar

2 carrots, grated

handful each of fresh coriander/ cilantro, mint and basil

iceberg lettuce and deep-fried shallots (see page 51), to serve

GARLIC PASTE

4 garlic cloves, unpeeled

½ teaspoon salt

1 shallot, finely chopped

2 lemon grass stalks, roughly chopped

1 tablespoon chopped fresh ginger

1 red chilli/chile

1 tablespoon toasted sesame seeds

CHILLI DRESSING

1 large red chilli/chile, chopped

1 red bird's eye chilli/chile, deseeded and chopped

1 garlic clove, crushed

2 tablespoons grated palm sugar/ jaggery

2 tablespoons fish sauce

grated zest and freshly squeezed juice 1 lime

Serves 4

Unlike those of its neighbours, Lao cuisine tends to be sour and salty rather than sweet, sour and salty, like this one. The addition of the roasted tomato salsa adds a fiery heat to the soup and a light smokey flavour.

HOT & SOUR FISH SOUP

First, make the jeow marg leng. Heat a stovetop ridged grill pan over a medium heat until smoking and then grill the tomatoes for 15–20 minutes until completely charred and softened. Set aside to cool, then peel and discard the blackened skin. Repeat with the garlic cloves, whole shallot and chillies, cooking them until the skins are charred and the flesh softened. Allow them to cool, then peel and discard the skins. Chop the vegetables and put in a pestle and mortar. Pound to a rough paste.

Transfer the paste to a mixing bowl and stir in the sugar, spring onion, coriander, lime juice and fish sauce. Store in a sterilized glass jar in the fridge for up to 3 weeks.

Soak the noodles in a bowlful of hot water for 10 minutes until softened. Drain well, shake dry and set aside.

Put the lime leaves, chilli, ginger, lemon grass and garlic in a pestle and mortar and pound together until fragrant – it should still be quite bitty. Transfer this paste to a saucepan set over a medium heat and pour over the stock. Bring to the boil, then simmer gently for 20 minutes until really fragrant.

Add the shallots and simmer for 5 minutes, then carefully add the fish fillets and cook gently for 4–5 minutes until cooked through. Remove the pan from the heat and stir in the spinach, jeow marg leng, lime juice, fish sauce and coriander. Cover with a lid and set aside for 5 minutes to allow the flavours to develop.

Divide the noodles between bowls and carefully spoon the fish on top, pour over the soup and serve at once with extra jeow marg leng.

200 g/7 oz. glass (cellophane) noodles

6 kaffir lime leaves, torn

1 large red chilli/chile, roughly chopped

2.5-cm/1-in. piece fresh ginger, peeled and chopped

1 lemon grass stalk, trimmed and roughly chopped

2 garlic cloves

1.5 litres/quarts chicken stock

2 shallots, finely chopped

500 g/1 lb. 2 oz. fish steaks or fillets, such as striped bass or bream

50 g/1 cup spinach, torn

4 tablespoons jeow marg leng (see below), plus extra to serve

freshly squeezed juice of 1 lime

2 tablespoons fish sauce

bunch of fresh coriander/cilantro

JEOW MARG LENG

6 large cherry/grape tomatoes

6 garlic cloves, unpeeled

1 large shallot, unpeeled

1–2 small red bird's eye chillies/chiles

½ teaspoon caster/granulated sugar

1 spring onion/scallion, finely chopped

1 tablespoon chopped fresh coriander/cilantro

2 teaspoons freshly squeezed lime juice

1 teaspoon fish sauce

Serves 4

This is traditionally a vegetarian dish served in a single bowl. It is often made with more than one type of grain and always includes a great balance of carbs, protein and vegetables. Here tofu makes up the protein element cooked to a crunch with a rich oyster sauce. The rice can be of any variety and choose your favourite vegetables to roast.

BUDDHA BOWLS with caramelized tofu

Preheat the oven to 200° (400°F) Gas 6. Cut the tofu into 2.5-cm/1-in. cubes and place in a bowl. Add the garlic, ginger, oyster sauce, soy sauce and honey, stir well and marinate for 30 minutes.

Cook the rice according to the packet instructions. Keep warm.

Place all the prepared vegetables on a roasting tray. Add the oil, soy sauce and sesame seeds and roast for 10–15 minutes until al dente.

Make the dressing. Put the chilli, garlic and salt in a pestle and mortar (or small blender) and pound well to form a rough paste. Transfer to a bowl and stir in the coriander, palm sugar, fish sauce and lime juice and stir until the sugar is dissolved.

Heat the oil in a wok or heavy saucepan and fry the marinated tofu pieces for 4–5 minutes unti golden and crunchy.

Divide the rice between bowls and top with the tofu, roasted vegetables, salad leaves and herbs and drizzle over the dressing.

250 g/9 oz. firm tofu

1 garlic clove, crushed

1 teaspoon grated fresh ginger

1 tablespoon oyster sauce

1 tablespoon light soy sauce

1 teaspoon clear honey

200 g/1 cup medium-grain brown rice

250 g/9 oz. mixed prepared vegetables such as baby carrots, broccoli florets, asparagus spears, sliced red (bell) pepper, courgette/zuccini slices, etc

1 tablespoon vegetable oil, plus extra for frying the tofu

2 teaspoons dark soy sauce

1 tablespoon sesame seeds

baby salad leaves and Asian herbs, to serve

BUDDHA BOWL DRESSING

1 green bird's eye chilli/chile, deseeded and roughly chopped

2 garlic cloves, chopped

a pinch of salt

1 tablespoon chopped fresh coriander/cilantro

2 tablespoons grated palm sugar/ jaggery

2 tablespoons fish sauce

2 tablespoons freshly squeezed lime juice

Serves 2

Szechuan is a province of China famous for its bold flavours, especially the pungent Szechuan peppercorn, which adds a delightful aromatic spiciness to dishes. Here it is used simply with beef strips and egg noodles.

SZECHUAN BEEF NOODLES

Start by making the sauce. Put all the ingredients in a bowl and stir well to dissolve the sesame paste. Set aside.

Put the sliced beef in a bowl with the soy sauce and set aside to marinate for at least 15 minutes.

Put 2 tablespoons of the oil in a wok set over a medium heat and stir-fry the marinated beef with its soy, in batches, for 3–4 minutes until browned. Remove the beef from the wok using a slotted spoon and set aside.

Add the remaining oil to the wok and fry the onion, garlic and ginger for 5 minutes. Stir in the sauce and peppercorns. Simmer for 5 minutes before returning the beef to the pan. Stir well and keep warm.

Meanwhile, cook the noodles by plunging them into a large saucepan of boiling water. Return to the boil and cook for 2–3 minutes until al dente. Drain well and divide among warmed plates. Spoon the beef mixture over the top and garnish with spring onions and coriander.

300 g/10½ oz. sliced beef fillet

2 tablespoons dark soy sauce

4 tablespoons sunflower oil

1 small onion, finely chopped

2 garlic cloves, crushed

2.5-cm/1-in. piece of fresh ginger, grated

1 teaspoon Szechuan peppercorns, toasted and ground

200 g/7 oz. dried egg noodles

SAUCE

200 ml/¾ cup hot chicken stock

50 ml/scant ¼ cup Shaoxing rice wine

2 tablespoons light soy sauce

2 tablespoons brown rice vinegar

1 tablespoon Asian sesame paste

2 teaspoons caster/granulated sugar

GARNISHES

2 spring onions/scallions, thinly sliced

a few sprigs of fresh coriander/ cilantro

Serves 4

Peanuts can be added to lots of dishes to add texture and make every bite crunchy and rich. Here, they contrast with the very silky glass (cellophane) noodles, and each and every simple and modest ingredient stands out.

STIR-FRIED NOODLES & BEANSPROUTS

To make the dipping sauce, crush the chilli into the soy sauce with the back of a spoon. Set aside until needed.

Put the noodles in a bowl, cover with warm water and allow to soak for 30 minutes. After 30 minutes, cut them into shorter lengths.

Heat the oil in a frying pan/skillet over a low–medium heat and fry the shallots for about 5 minutes. Add the noodles, soy sauce, pepper and bouillon, if using, and stir-fry for 2–3 minutes.

Add the chilli, wine and beansprouts. Stir-fry for 2 minutes, then remove from the heat and mix in the garlic chives, coriander and peanuts. Serve hot or at room temperature with the dipping sauce.

200 g/7 oz. glass (cellophane) noodles

a dash of cooking oil

2 Asian shallots, finely chopped

3 tablespoons light soy sauce

a pinch of black pepper

a pinch of pork or vegetable bouillon (optional)

1 bird's eye chilli/chile, thinly sliced

100 ml/scant ½ cup white wine or water

160 g/2⅓ cups beansprouts

a handful of garlic chives, cut into 2.5-cm/1-in. lengths, or garden mint (optional)

2 sprigs of fresh coriander/cilantro, chopped

2 big tablespoons roasted salted peanuts, crushed

DIPPING SAUCE (OPTIONAL)

1 bird's eye chilli/chile, sliced

3 tablespoons soy sauce

Serves 2

This dish is super healthy and quick to prepare, plus full of punchy flavours. The perfect no-fuss meal for hungry people! Japanese cuisine tends to be mild on the whole, but this dish has a real kick to it. The earthiness of the soba noodles mixed with the chilli will lift your spirits and boost your energy on a cold day.

SPICY MISO SOBA NOODLE SOUP
with ginger teriyaki tofu

For the ginger teriyaki tofu, wrap the tofu in plenty of paper towels and compress under a heavy kitchen utensil for 30 minutes to remove excess water.

Dice the tofu into cubes. In a medium frying pan/skillet, heat the vegetable oil over a medium heat and fry the tofu until browned on all sides. Add the ginger and stir in. Add the soy sauce and mirin and fry for 2 minutes until the tofu becomes caramelized. Set aside.

For the noodle soup, put the vegetable oil in a saucepan over a medium heat. Add the garlic and spring onions and fry for 1 minute to infuse some flavour into the oil.

Add the dashi and bring to the boil. Once boiling, turn down the heat and simmer for 5 minutes.

Meanwhile, cook the dried soba noodles in a separate pan of boiling water following the packet instructions. Drain well and divide between serving bowls.

Combine the red miso and gochujang in a cup and stir in a ladleful of the dashi until dissolved. Add the miso mixture back into the saucepan with the soup and stir well to combine. Heat through for another minute, if needed, before serving.

Pour the hot miso soup over the cooked soba noodles in the serving bowls, then top with the ginger teriyaki tofu, wakame, sesame seeds, dried chilli strips and spring onion, if liked.

GINGER TERIYAKI TOFU

200 g/7 oz. firm tofu

1 tablespoon vegetable oil

1 teaspoon peeled and very finely chopped fresh ginger

2 tablespoons soy sauce

2 tablespoons mirin

NOODLE SOUP

1 tablespoon vegetable oil

2 garlic cloves, finely chopped

2 spring onions/scallions, whites only, finely chopped

800 ml/3⅓ cups dashi broth (see page 44)

160 g/5½ oz. dried soba (buckwheat) noodles

3 tablespoons red miso

1 tablespoon gochujang

TO SERVE (OPTIONAL)

2 tablespoons dried wakame seaweed, soaked in water to reconstitute, then drained

1 tablespoon toasted mixed black and white sesame seeds

dried red chilli/chile strips

1 spring onion/scallion, thinly sliced

Serves 2

Singapore is famous for its chilli crab and it is always such a treat to make this at home. The crab needs to be very fresh when cooked and this does require some effort, but it is so worth it! Alternatively, you can substitute the crab for 1 kg/2¼ lb. of unshelled tiger prawn/jumbo shrimp. The fun is in the mess that this makes – serve the seafood in its shell and everyone can dig in. The coconut rice is the perfect vehicle for all the juices.

CHILLI CRAB & COCONUT RICE

Whisk the cornflour and 200 ml/scant 1 cup water in a small bowl to combine and set aside.

Process the chillies and onion in a food processor until a paste forms and set aside.

Heat the vegetable oil in a large wok over a medium heat. Add the crab and stir-fry until it starts to colour. Remove the crab using a slotted spoon and set aside. You'll be using the wok again.

Meanwhile, for the coconut rice, place all the ingredients except the rice in a saucepan and bring to a simmer over a medium–high heat. Add the rice and stir until it returns to the simmer. Cover, reduce the heat to very low and cook for 15–20 minutes until the rice is tender. Remove from the heat and allow to stand for 5 minutes.

Add the chilli paste to the wok over a medium–high heat and stir until tender. Add the ginger and garlic and stir until fragrant. Add the tomato purée and stir until the mixture darkens in colour. Add the fresh tomatoes and sriracha and 100 ml/scant ½ cup water. Bring to a simmer, then add the cornflour mixture and stir to combine. Add the crab and cook, stirring occasionally, until orange and cooked through. Drizzle in the egg and stir to coat. Season to taste with soy sauce, fish sauce, sugar and salt. Serve hot with coriander, spring onions, lime wedges and the coconut rice.

½ teaspoon cornflour/cornstarch
3 red long chillies/chiles
1 onion, finely chopped
80 ml/⅓ cup vegetable oil
2 crabs (jointed by your fishmonger)
thumb-sized piece of fresh ginger, grated
3 garlic cloves, crushed
1 tablespoon tomato purée/paste
6 tomatoes, roughly chopped
1 tablespoon sriracha
1 egg, lightly beaten
2 tablespoons light soy sauce
1 tablespoon fish sauce
1–2 tablespoons palm sugar/jaggery
salt

COCONUT RICE
400 ml/1¾ cups coconut milk
200 ml/scant 1 cup fresh young coconut water
1 teaspoon each cumin and coriander seeds, finely ground in a mortar and pestle
1 teaspoon fish paste
2 lemon grass stalks, white part only, finely chopped
1 teaspoon salt
400 g/2¼ cups jasmine rice, rinsed

TO SERVE
fresh coriander/cilantro
thinly sliced spring onions/scallions
lime wedges

Serves 4–6

Pecel is a peanut sauce from Java in Indonesia and is traditionally served with carbs. So serving on a dish of rice with vegetables is perfect. This is very similar to a regular nasi goreng, but the use of pecel sauce adds a lovely rich nuttiness to the dish.

VEGETABLE NASI GORENG with pecel sauce

Start by making the pecel sauce. Heat the oil in a small frying pan/skillet. Add the chillies, garlic and ginger and cook gently for 5 minutes until they are soft but not browned. Set aside to cool completely.

Pound the peanuts in a pestle and mortar (or use a small food processor) until a smooth paste is formed. Transfer to a bowl and wipe the pestle and mortar clean. Add the chilli mixture, including the oil it was cooked in, to the pestle and mortar and pound until smooth. Add the tamarind, sugar and salt and pound again until the paste is as smooth as possible. Stir in the peanuts to make a thick paste-like sauce. Set aside.

Boil the eggs in a saucepan of boiling water for 6 minutes, then remove the eggs and plunge into cold water. As soon as they are cool enough to handle, peel the eggs. Cut the eggs in half.

Heat 2 tablespoons of the oil in a wok (or large frying pan) and stir-fry the vegetables until they are al dente. Remove from the pan and wipe the pan clean. Add the remaining oil to the pan. Add the turmeric, stir well and then add the rice, soy sauce and ketjap manis. Stir-fry for 2–3 minutes until the rice is heated through. Return the vegetables to the pan and stir to combine. Cook through for 1 minute.

Divide the rice mixture among bowls and top each one with an egg half, some sesame seeds and a spoonful of the peanut sauce. Serve with lime wedges.

2 eggs

3 tablespoons vegetable oil

350 g/12 oz. prepared mixed vegetables, such as red onion, carrots, celery, green beans, red (bell) peppers, pak choi/bok choy and spring onions/scallions

½ teaspoon ground turmeric

800 g/5¾ cups cooked white long-grain rice, cooled and chilled (see page 7)

2 tablespoons light soy sauce

1 tablespoon ketjap manis

PECEL SAUCE

1 tablespoon vegetable oil

2 large red chillies/chiles, deseeded and chopped

1 red bird's eye chillies/chiles, deseeded and chopped

2 garlic cloves, crushed

2-cm/1-in. piece of fresh ginger, peeled and grated

65 g/½ cup whole raw peanuts

1 teaspoon tamarind paste

25 g/1 oz. palm sugar/jaggery, grated or soft brown sugar

1 teaspoon sea salt

GARNISHES

toasted sesame seeds

lime wedges

Serves 4

UMAMI RICH

In all Asian dishes you will find a lovely balance of strong and delicate flavours. Here we have the richness of pork belly, the mellow flavour of noodles, the zing of pickled vegetables and finally a sweet, sour dressing.

BBQ PORK NOODLE BOWLS with dipping sauce

Place the pork belly in a shallow dish. Whisk the fish sauce, ketjap manis, five-spice, pepper and garlic cloves together, and pour over the pork. Cover and set in the fridge to marinate overnight.

Preheat the oven to 180°C (350°F) Gas 4.

Transfer the pork belly to the prepared roasting pan and roast in the preheated oven for 1 hour, turning halfway through, until the pork is golden, sticky and tender. Leave to cool for 30 minutes until just warm and cut into pieces.

Meanwhile, put the noodles in a bowl, cover with boiling water and soak for 30 minutes until softened. Drain the noodles, pat dry and divide among serving bowls. Arrange the pork, beansprouts, lettuce leaves, herbs and pickled vegetables on plates around the table for people to help themselves. Serve with a bowl of nuoc cham.

500 g/1 lb. 2 oz. pork belly strips, each cut into 3 pieces

3 tablespoons fish sauce

2 tablespoons ketjap manis

1 teaspoon Chinese five-spice powder

½ teaspoon freshly ground black pepper

4 garlic cloves, crushed

250 g/9 oz. dried rice stick noodles

125 g/2⅓ cups beansprouts, trimmed

8–12 cup-shaped leaves from an iceberg/butter lettuce

a selection of fresh herbs, such as mint, coriander/cilantro and Thai basil

pickled vegetables

1 quantity nuoc cham (see page 51)

a roasting pan lined with baking parchment

Serves 4

A bed of black rice topped with white fish and mushrooms, this is a simple and elegant dish, gently flavoured with a Japanese inspired miso-ginger dressing.

BLACK & WHITE BOWL

Place the rinsed rice, salt and 1 litre/quart water in a saucepan and set aside to soak for 1 hour. Bring the pan to a simmer, then reduce the heat to low, cover with a tight-fitting lid and cook without uncovering for 25 minutes. Remove the pan from the heat and stand covered for 10 minutes, then stir in soy sauce, mirin, rice vinegar and sesame seeds.

For the white miso dressing, whisk the miso, vinegar and lemon juice in a bowl to combine, then whisk in the oils, ginger and garlic. Thin with a little water if necessary to achieve a drizzling consistency.

Meanwhile, heat a frying pan/skillet to medium heat, add 1 tablespoon of the sesame oil and sauté the chestnut mushrooms for a few minutes (just to soften), then add the enoki for another few minutes and set aside. Wipe the pan out ready for the cod.

Brush the cod with the white miso and remaining tablespoon of sesame oil. Heat the pan to a medium heat, then add the cod and cook, without moving it at all, for about 2–3 minutes or until the skin is golden and crisp. If you are cooking without the skin, the fish should also be golden. Carefully turn the cod over to cook the other side until the fish is cooked through.

Divide the warm rice between serving bowls, top with the cod and cooking juices, cabbage and mushrooms. Drizzle generously with the white miso dressing, scatter with extra sesame seeds, spring onions and iceplant leaves or samphire (if using) and serve.

400 g/generous 2 cups black rice, rinsed

1 teaspoon salt

2 tablespoons soy sauce

2 teaspoons mirin

2 teaspoons rice vinegar

1 tablespoon mixed black and white sesame seeds, plus extra to serve

2 tablespoons sesame oil

200 g/7 oz. chestnut/cremini mushrooms

60 g/2 oz. enoki mushrooms, trimmed

2 x cod fillets, skin on (approx 200 g/7 oz. each)

2 tablespoons white miso

150 g/5½ oz. white cabbage, very thinly shaved on a mandoline

spring onions/scallions, thinly sliced, to serve

edible iceplant leaves or samphire, to garnish (optional)

WHITE MISO DRESSING

1 tablespoon shiro miso

1 tablespoon rice vinegar

1 tablespoon freshly squeezed lemon juice

2 tablespoons vegetable oil

2 teaspoons sesame oil

1 teaspoon finely grated ginger

½ garlic clove, finely grated

Serves 2

With this dish, you will see whether you have true Japanese taste! The rice is topped with sticky natto (fermented soy beans), and in Japan this is called a 'neba neba' texture. The onsen tamago or 'hot springs egg' served on top of this rice bowl is an egg slowly poached in warm water, which gives a soft silky white and custard-like yolk.

FERMENTED SOY BEANS ON RICE

First, make the tsuyu sauce. Combine both soy sauces, the mirin, sake and brown sugar in a small saucepan. Add the kombu and leave to cold-soak for 30 minutes.

To make the onsen tamago eggs, place 1.2 litres/quarts of water in the saucepan (this will be enough to submerge the eggs). Bring to the boil. Add 200 ml/generous ¾ cup cold water to the pan and turn off the heat. Add the eggs in gently, then cover with a lid. Leave the eggs to slow-poach for 18 minutes in the residual heat.

Drain and then gently rinse the eggs under cold running water to stop the cooking process completely. Drain again. Set aside.

Place the okra on a chopping board and sprinkle with the sea salt. Use your palms to roll the okra in the salt, this will help to remove the hairy surface and makes the colour bright green.

Bring some water to the boil in a saucepan and boil the salted okra for 2 minutes. Rinse under cold running water to stop the cooking process and drain. Slice the okra thinly and set aside.

Stir the natto (fermented soy beans) inside their packets to create the 'neba neba' texture (almost sticky, slimy and stringy).

To serve, portion the cooked rice into serving bowls. Crack the shells of the onsen tamago eggs open and top each rice bowl with an egg, half the natto and okra, radishes, avocado and toasted pine nuts. Finish with a drizzle of tsuyu sauce over the top and some shredded nori seaweed.

2 eggs

4 okra

¼ tsp sea salt

2 x 40-g/1½-oz. packets of natto (fermented soy beans)

400 g/3 cups cooked Japanese rice of your choice

4 small red radishes, very thinly sliced

1 ripe avocado, diced

2 tbsp pine nuts, toasted

1 tbsp Tsuyu Sauce (see below)

1 sheet of nori seaweed, shredded

TSUYU SAUCE

100 ml/scant ½ cup soy sauce

50 ml/3½ tablespoons light soy sauce

100 ml/scant ½ cup mirin

50 ml/3½ tablespoons sake

1 tablespoon soft light brown sugar

5 x 5-cm/2 x 2-in. piece of kombu

Serves 2

Wild garlic has a great affinity with Asian flavourings, such as ginger, soy sauce and Japanese miso paste. Cooked in just minutes and served simply with rice or noodles, this pork dish makes a perfect midweek supper. If you wish, tofu could be used instead of pork.

WILD GARLIC MISO PORK STIR-FRY

Heat a wok until hot. Add the oil and heat through. Add the ginger and fry briefly, stirring, until fragrant.

Add the pork strips and fry, stirring, until lightened. Pour in the rice wine and allow to sizzle briefly. Add the soy sauce and miso paste and stir-fry for 2–3 minutes.

Add the wild garlic and stir-fry until just wilted. Check the pork has cooked through and serve.

VARIATION: For a vegetarian version of the dish, cube 400 g/14 oz. of firm tofu and pat dry. Add to the wok once the ginger is fragrant and stir-fry for 2–3 minutes until the tofu takes on a little colour. Proceed with the recipe as directed.

1 tablespoon sunflower or vegetable oil

1-cm/$\frac{1}{2}$-in. piece fresh ginger, peeled and finely chopped

400 g/14 oz. lean pork fillet, sliced into 1-cm/$\frac{1}{2}$-in. strips

1 tablespoon rice wine or Amontillado sherry

1 tablespoon dark soy sauce

1 tablespoon dark miso paste

40 g/1$\frac{1}{2}$ oz. wild garlic leaves/ ramps, rinsed well and chopped into 2.5-cm/1-in. lengths

Serves 4

This is a light, delicately flavoured mushroom soup. Vegetarians may want to use a version of dashi without the bonito flakes. You should be able to buy most of the mushrooms fairly readily from larger supermarkets or online, but could substitute like for like with any mushrooms you are able to find.

MUSHROOM UDON

Plunge the noodles into a saucepan of boiling water and cook for about 4–5 minutes, or until al dente. Drain, refresh under cold water and shake dry. Set aside.

Pour the broth, soy sauce, mirin and sake into a saucepan set over a medium heat and bring to the boil. Add the mushrooms except the enoki and simmer gently for 5 minutes until the mushrooms are tender. Stir in the sugar snap peas and enoki mushrooms and simmer for a further 2 minutes.

Divide the noodles among warmed bowls and top with the tofu and seaweed, pour over the soup and serve at once, sprinkled with seven-spice powder.

200 g/7 oz. dried udon noodles

1.5 litres/quarts dashi broth (see page 44)

50 ml/scant ¼ cup dark soy sauce

3 tablespoons mirin

2 tablespoons sake

500 g/1 lb. 2 oz. mixed mushrooms, including shiitake, oyster and enoki

150 g/1 cup sugar snap peas, trimmed and cut in half lengthways

200 g/2 cups cubed silken/ soft tofu

2 tablespoons dried wakame seaweed

seven-spice powder, to serve

Serves 4

Banh mi is the name for a Vietnamese barbecued pork and vegetable sub (baguette) served as street food. Here it is adapted into an equally delicious pork rice bowl.

BANH MI RICE BOWL

Place the pork belly strips in a bowl. Combine the pork marinade ingredients and pour over the pork strips, turning to coat thoroughly. Leave to marinate for 30 minutes.

Cook the rice according to the packet instructions. Keep warm.

Heat the oil in a heavy-based frying pan/skillet over a high heat and fry the marinated pork strips, in batches, for 2 minutes each side until charred. Cool for a few minutes, then slice thinly.

Divide the rice among bowls and arrange the pork and easy pickles on top along with the salad leaves and fresh herbs. Serve with sweet chilli sauce and crispy shallots.

600 g/1 lb. 5 oz. pork belly strips, skin removed

400 g/2¼ cups jasmine rice

2 tablespoons vegetable oil

1 quantity easy pickles (see page 94)

handful of salad leaves

a few fresh coriander, mint and basil leaves

sweet chilli sauce and deep-fried shallots (see page 51), to serve

PORK MARINADE

2½ tablespoons hoisin sauce

2 tablespoons honey

4 tablespoons light soy sauce

1 tablespoon Shaoxing wine

½ teaspoon sesame oil

½ teaspoon Chinese five-spice

Serves 4

Most Asian countries make some sort of large seafood hotpot and this is based on a Malaysian version.

SEAFOOD STEAMBOAT

Soak the noodles in a bowlful of hot water for about 10–20 minutes until softened.

Drain well, shake dry and set aside.

Pour the stock into a large saucepan set over a medium heat. Add the fish sauce and sugar and bring to the boil. Once boiling, reduce the heat but keep warm.

Next prepare the seafood. Remove any bones from the fish and cut into 2.5-cm/1-in. cubes. Open out the squid body by cutting down one side and score the inside flesh with a sharp knife in a diamond pattern. Cut into 2.5-cm/1-in. pieces.

Peel the prawns, leaving the tail section intact. Cut down the back of each one almost in half and pull out the black intestinal tract. Wash the prawns, dry and set aside.

Trim the grey muscle from the side of each scallop and set aside.

Arrange all the seafood, cooked noodles and the choi sum on a large platter on the table.

Place a portable gas burner in the middle of the table and pour half the chicken stock into a smaller saucepan. Bring to a gentle simmer (keeping the remaining stock warm on the stove). Place the bowls of garnishes next to each guest along with a serving bowl and noodles.

Using tongs, the guests can then cook the seafood and choi sum in the hot stock, which will become increasingly flavoursome. As the food cooks, spoon it into the serving bowls with some noodles and a little of the stock and top with fresh herbs, chillies and lime juice. Top up with more stock as required.

350 g/11½ oz. dried rice vermicelli noodles
2 litres/3½ pints chicken stock
4 tablespoons fish sauce
2 tablespoons grated palm sugar/jaggery
250 g/9 oz. skinless white fish fillets, such as cod, ling or pollock
250 g/9 oz. cleaned squid bodies
250 g/3¾ cups (about 25) prawns/shrimp
250 g/9 oz. (about 15) scallops
250 g/9 oz. (about 25) fresh clams (or about 10 mussels), cleaned
125 g/1½ cups choi sum (Chinese broccoli)

TO SERVE
a handful each of fresh Thai basil, mint and coriander/cilantro
red chillies/chiles, sliced
2 limes, cut into wedges

Serves 6

Just about my favourite Asian dish of all time. I can't really add to that. This recipe includes a homemade red curry sauce, which I recommend you make as it has a far fresher and more fragrant flavour than most bought pastes. Once made it keeps well in the fridge for up to a month or can be frozen.

DUCK RED CURRY over rice

Preheat the oven to 200°C (400°F) Gas 6. Cook the rice according to the packet instructions and keep warm.

Make the red curry paste. Place the whole spices in a dry frying pan/skillet and heat for 2 minutes until they darken in colour and start to give off an aroma. Cool, then grind to a powder in a spice grinder. In a pestle and mortar pound together the garlic cloves, lemon grass, fresh and dried chillies, galangal, lime zest and shrimp paste. Combine with the toasted spices and grind to form a really smooth paste. Alternatively, use a blender.

Season the duck breasts, rubbing the salt and Szechuan pepper well into the skin. Place the duck, skin-side down, in a cold frying pan and place over a medium heat. Cook for 5 minutes until the skin is golden and crispy and the fat released, then transfer to a roasting pan and roast for a further 8 minutes. Remove from the oven and let rest for 10 minutes, then slice thinly.

Meanwhile, heat the oil in a wok. Add 3–4 tablespoons of the red curry paste and fry for 2–3 minutes until it splits. Add the coconut milk, stock, palm sugar, fish sauce and lime leaves and bring to the boil. Simmer for 5 minutes until thickened. Add the lime juice.

Divide the rice among bowls and top each one with slices of duck. Serve topped with fresh herbs, sliced red chillies and beansprouts.

400 g/2¼ cups jasmine rice

2 medium duck breast fillets (about 350 g/12 oz. each), scored

1 teaspoon sea salt

1 teaspoon Szechuan peppercorns, roughly ground

2 tablespoons vegetable oil

400 ml/1⅔ cup coconut milk

300 ml/1¼ cups chicken stock

3 tablespoons grated palm sugar/ jaggery

3 tablespoons Thai fish sauce

4 lime leaves, chopped

3 tablespoons freshly squeezed lime juice

fresh herbs, sliced red chilli/chile and beansprouts, to serve

RED CURRY PASTE

1 teaspoon white peppercorns

2 teaspoons cumin seeds

1 teaspoon coriander seeds

6 star anise

3 cinnamon sticks

1 garlic bulb

2 lemon grass stalks, chopped

2 long red chillies/chiles, chopped

6 dried red chillies/chiles, deseeded and crumbled

2 tablespoons chopped galangal (or 1 tablespoon grated root ginger)

grated zest of 1 kaffir lime

3 tablespoons shrimp paste

Serves 4

'Khmer noodles' is the generic name given to num banh chok, a classic Cambodian soup traditionally served at breakfast or as an afternoon snack. Although you will find regional differences, it is always made with a freshly pounded lemon grass paste, fish, noodles and a selection of crisp raw vegetables and fresh herbs.

NUM BANH CHOK

Soak the noodles in a bowlful of hot water for 20 minutes until softened. Drain well using a kitchen cloth and set aside.

To make the lemon grass paste, discard the hard end of the lemon grass stalk and peel away and discard the hard outer leaves until you reach the soft core of the stalk. Trim lengths of about 5 cm/2 in. and roughly chop the remaining core. Place the lemon grass in a food processor with the remaining ingredients and blend to a smooth paste.

Heat the oil in a wok or saucepan set over a medium heat until it starts to shimmer. Add the lemon grass paste and fry for 2–3 minutes until fragrant. Add the fish pieces and fry gently for 2 minutes until cooked. Remove the fish from the pan as carefully as you can and set aside.

Add the stock, coconut cream and coconut milk to the pan and simmer gently for 10 minutes until thick and creamy. Stir in the fish sauce and sugar and simmer for a final minute.

Divide the noodles among bowls and top with the pieces of fish. Pour over the broth and serve with bowls of sliced cucumber, beansprouts and lotus root, if using, for topping.

250 g/9 oz. dried rice stick noodles
2 tablespoons vegetable oil
350 g/11 oz. bream or snapper fillets, cut into 2.5-cm/1-in. pieces
250 ml/1 cup chicken stock
125 ml/½ cup coconut cream
125 ml/½ cup coconut milk
1 tablespoon fish sauce
2 teaspoons grated palm sugar/ jaggery

LEMON GRASS PASTE
6 lemon grass stalks
2.5-cm/1-in. piece fresh galangal, peeled and roughly chopped
2.5-cm/1-in. piece fresh turmeric, peeled and roughly chopped
2 kaffir lime leaves, shredded
2 garlic cloves, roughly chopped
2 tablespoons chopped peanuts
1 teaspoon shrimp paste
1 teaspoon freshly grated ginger

TO SERVE
½ cucumber, sliced
60 g/1 cup beansprouts
lotus root (optional)

Serves 4

Tamarind is one of the ingredients used in South-east Asia to impart the sour flavour for which the cuisine is renowned. Here, paired with the prawns, asparagus and crab, it is quite delightful.

PRAWN, CRAB & TAMARIND RICE NOODLES

Soak the noodles in a bowlful of hot water for 10–20 minutes until softened. Drain well, shake dry and set aside in a large mixing bowl.

To make the sauce, whisk all the ingredients together in a small mixing bowl, stirring well to dissolve the sugar. Set aside.

Heat the oil in a wok or large frying pan/skillet set over a medium–high heat. Add the garlic, stir-fry for 10 seconds and then add the onion and pepper. Stir-fry for 2 minutes, then add the prawns and asparagus and continue to stir-fry for 2 minutes until the prawns are cooked through.

Add the crab meat and tamarind sauce and cook for 2 minutes. Add the noodles, spring onions and coriander, stir-fry until the noodles are heated through and serve immediately with extra coriander sprinkled on top.

NOTE: Tamarind can be bought whole in pods, as a block of hard pulp or as a concentrate. To make tamarind water, dilute the concentrate three parts to one part water and use as instructed.

200 g/7 oz. glass (cellophane) noodles
2 tablespoons peanut oil
4 garlic cloves, sliced
1 red onion, sliced
½ tablespoon freshly ground black pepper
350 g/4¼ cups (about 35) raw prawns/shrimp, peeled, deveined and butterflied
350 g/3 cups asparagus tips, trimmed and cut into 5-cm/2-in. pieces
250 g/½ cup picked fresh crab meat
2 spring onions/scallions, sliced
4 tablespoons chopped fresh coriander/cilantro, plus extra to serve

TAMARIND SAUCE
125 ml/½ cup tamarind water (see Note left)
2 tablespoons fish sauce
2 tablespoons grated palm sugar/ jaggery

Serves 4

Burmese food is full of influences from its neighbouring countries and their cultures, but also present are Indian influences like spices and chickpea/gram flour used as a thickening agent. Mohinga is an aromatic noodle soup served mainly for breakfast. In fact Mohinga is considered by many as Myanmar's national dish and is served at hawkers' stalls all over the country.

MOHINGA

Soak the noodles in a bowlful of hot water for 10–20 minutes until softened. Drain well, shake dry and set aside.

Grind the lemon grass, garlic, ginger, shrimp paste and fish sauce together in a pestle and mortar or food processor to form a thin paste.

Heat the oil in a saucepan set over a medium heat and gently fry the onion and banana stem, if using (leave the palm hearts until a little later, if using), for 5 minutes until softened. Stir in the turmeric and chilli flakes and cook for 1 minute. Add the lemon grass paste and fry for a further 5 minutes.

Add the minced fish and cook, stirring continuously, until golden. Pour in the stock and bring to the boil.

Meanwhile, combine the toasted chickpea flour with 2 tablespoons cold water in a bowl until smooth. Stir in 3–4 tablespoons of the hot stock and then whisk the whole lot back into the soup. Bring to the boil, stirring continuously, and simmer for 5 minutes.

Divide the noodles among serving bowls. Spoon over the soup and serve with a platter of the garnishes.

200 g/7 oz. dried rice vermicelli noodles
1 lemon grass stalk, trimmed and finely chopped
2 garlic cloves, roughly chopped
2 teaspoons freshly grated ginger
1 teaspoon shrimp paste
1 tablespoon fish sauce
3 tablespoons vegetable oil
1 onion, thinly sliced
50 g/2 oz. banana stem or canned palm heart, sliced (optional)
1 teaspoon ground turmeric
¼ teaspoon dried red chilli/ hot red pepper flakes
250 g/9 oz. skinless white fish fillet, finely chopped or minced
1.25 litres/quarts chicken stock
40 g/½ cup chickpea/gram flour, toasted

GARNISHES
2 hard-boiled/hard-cooked eggs, peeled and finely chopped
2 tablespoons deep-fried shallots (see page 51)
2 tablespoons sambal olek

Serves 4

Every now and then a cookbook comes along that spends weeks next to my bed so I can read it nightly, absorbing the recipes to use at a later date. This happened with a book called 'Ivan Ramen', by an American ramen aficionado. The story is fascinating and the recipes inspirational. This is inspired by one such recipe, albeit a shorter version.

SHIO RAMEN with pork & eggs

Pour the sake and mirin into a small saucepan set over a medium heat and bring slowly to the boil. Add the garlic, ginger, dark and light soy sauces and the sugar. Stir until the sugar dissolves. Bring to the boil and simmer gently for 5 minutes. Remove from the heat and let cool.

Cut the pork belly in half across the grain to make two similar squares and put in a saucepan into which the pork fits snugly.

Pour over the cooled soy mixture, return to the heat and bring to the boil. Cover and simmer gently for 1 hour or until the pork is tender. Remove the pan from the heat but leave the pork in the stock to cool at room temperature. Remove the pork from the stock, reserving the stock, and cut into thick slices. Set aside.

Put the eggs in a saucepan of cold water and set over a high heat. Bring to the boil and simmer for 5 minutes. Remove the eggs from the pan and immediately rinse under cold running water until they are cool enough to handle. Peel the eggs and place them in a clean bowl. Pour over the reserved pork stock and leave to soak for 30 minutes. Lift the eggs from the stock and cut in half lengthways.

Meanwhile, bring the chicken stock to the boil in a large saucepan and simmer until reduced by about one-third to 1.25 litres/quarts. Remove from the heat and stir in 4 tablespoons of the reserved pork stock. Add the pork belly slices and warm through for 5 minutes.

Plunge the noodles into a saucepan of boiling water, return to the boil and cook for about 4 minutes or until al dente. Drain well, then divide the noodles among soup bowls. Spoon over the stock and pork slices, add 2 egg halves to each bowl and serve garnished with spring onions.

1 tablespoon sake
1 tablespoon mirin
1 garlic clove, crushed
1 teaspoon freshly grated ginger
50 ml/3½ tablespoons dark soy sauce
50 ml/3½ tablespoons light soy sauce
1 tablespoon caster/granulated sugar
750-g/1½-lb. piece of pork belly, skin removed
4 eggs
2 litres/quarts chicken stock
250 g/9 oz. dried ramen noodles
spring onions/scallions, thinly sliced, to garnish

Serves 4

Probably the best known of all Thai dishes, pad Thai in its simplest form is a basic combination of fried noodles with tofu, egg and beansprouts. Fresh cooked prawns/shrimp add a touch of luxury to the dish.

PRAWN PAD THAI

Soak the dried noodles in a bowlful of hot water for 20–30 minutes until softened. Drain well, pat dry with a clean kitchen cloth and set aside in a large mixing bowl.

Whisk all the sauce ingredients together in a small mixing bowl and set aside.

Heat 2 tablespoons of the oil in a wok or large frying pan/skillet set over a medium heat. Add the garlic and fry for 30 seconds, remove with a slotted spoon and set aside. Add the prawns to the pan and stir-fry for 2 minutes until cooked, remove with a slotted spoon and set aside.

Add the tofu to the pan (with a little more oil, if needed) and stir-fry for 4–5 minutes until crispy. Pour the beaten egg into the pan and cook, stirring gently until it sets around the tofu. Remove with a slotted spoon and break up roughly.

Add the remaining oil to the pan and stir-fry the spring onions and dried shrimp for 2 minutes until the onions are softened. Stir in the noodles, prawns, garlic, tofu mixture and the sauce, stirring constantly until everything is heated through. Stir through the beansprouts and coriander.

Transfer the noodles to serving dishes, sprinkle over the peanuts, cayenne pepper and coriander leaves, and serve with lime wedges and extra beansprouts.

250 g/9 oz. dried rice stick noodles

4 tablespoons peanut or vegetable oil

2 garlic cloves, sliced

24 raw prawns/shrimp, peeled and deveined

125 g/1 cup firm tofu, diced

2 eggs, lightly beaten

4 spring onions/ scallions, cut into 2.5-cm/1-in. lengths

1 tablespoon dried shrimp

125 g/2 cups beansprouts, trimmed, plus extra to serve

2 tablespoons chopped fresh coriander/ cilantro

SAUCE

2 tablespoons grated palm sugar/jaggery

2 tablespoons fish sauce

2 tablespoons freshly squeezed lime juice

1 tablespoon tamarind water (see page 148)

2 teaspoons light soy sauce

TO SERVE

peanuts, crushed

a pinch of cayenne pepper

fresh coriander/ cilantro leaves

lime wedges

Serves 4

To many westerners it seems rather bizarre to serve savoury porridge as a breakfast dish, but this is common in many Asian cultures. Don't be put off, rather make it for your lunch or dinner, it is so good.

CLAMS OVER RICE PORRIDGE
with ssamjang sauce

Make the stock. Dilute the dashi powder with 1.5 litres/quarts cold water. Place in a saucepan with the garlic, ginger, lime leaves, chilli and star anise. Bring to the boil, partially cover and simmer for 20 minutes. Strain and discard the aromatics.

Meanwhile, make the sauce. Place all the ingredients in a bowl and stir well until combined. Set aside.

Place a clean saucepan over a medium heat. Add the clams and 1 tablespoon of the dashi stock. Simmer, covered, for 5 minutes until all the clams have opened. Discard any that remain closed. Drain and refresh the clams under cold water. Drain again and set aside. Reserve the stock.

Add enough of the reserved dashi stock to the clam liquid to give you 1.25 litres/quarts in total. Add the fish sauce and sugar and return to a simmer. Stir in the rice, partially cover the pan and simmer gently, uncovered, for 20 minutes, stirring from time to time until the rice is al dente and the stock absorbed. Stir in the vinegar and remove the pan from the heat.

Stir in the clams, add the lid and rest for 2 minutes to reheat the clams. Divide amongst bowls and serve topped with the ssamjang sauce, coriander leaves and some crispy shallots.

750 g/1½ lb. clams, scrubbed
3 tablespoons fish sauce
3 tablespoons grated palm sugar/ jaggery
300 g/1½ cups jasmine rice
1½ tablespoons rice wine vinegar
fresh coriander/cilantro leaves and deep-fried shallots (see page 51), to serve

DASHI STOCK
2 sachets dashi powder
1 garlic clove, roughly chopped
5-cm/2-in. piece fresh ginger, thickly sliced
6 lime leaves, bashed
1 large red chilli/chile, bashed lightly
1 star anise, lightly bashed

SSAMJANG SAUCE
50 g/3½ tablespoons fermented soybean paste
2 teaspoons gochujang
1 spring onion/scallion, finely chopped
1 small garlic clove, crushed
1 small shallot, finely chopped
2 teaspoons rice wine vinegar
2 teaspoons sesame oil
1 teaspoon clear honey
1 teaspoon toasted sesame seeds
1 tablespoon sunflower oil

Serves 4

INDEX

CREDITS

RECIPES

Louise Pickford
All recipes by Louise Pickford (including some previously published in *The Noodle Bowl* 2020), with the exception of the those listed below:

Atsuko Ikeda
Chicken & Eggs on Rice
Chicken Teriyaki with Lime on Quinoa Rice
Fermented Soy Beans on Rice
Sichuan Tofu & Aubergine Rice Bowls
Simmered Beef & Tomatoes on Rice

Spicy Miso Soba Noodle Soup with Ginger Teriyaki Fish

Jackie Kearney
Fragrant Breakfast Soup with Rice

Kathy Kordalis
Bibimbap-y Bowl
Black & White Bowl
Chilli Crab & Coconut Rice
Chirashi-zushi
Dashi Rice Green Tea Broth Bowl
Miso Brown Rice Salad with Tofu & Ginger Dressing
Vietnamese-style Rice Bowl with Chicken Skewers & Nuoc Cham

Jenny Linford
Gochujang-glazed Mushroom & Whole Grain Rice Bowls
Thai-style Fish with Fried Garlic
Wild Garlic Miso Pork Stir-fry

Uyen Luu
Crab, Tomato & Omelette Soup
Hue Noodle Soup with Beef & Pork
Stir-fried Noodles & Beansprouts
Stir-fried Udon Noodles & Vegetables
Udon Noodle Soup with Fishcakes

PHOTOGRAPHY

All photography by Ian Wallace with food and prop styling by Louise Pickford, with the exception of:

Mowie Kay
Pages 12, 42, 62, 104, 124, 133.

Yuki Sugiura
Pages 19, 20, 76, 80, 123, 134.

Claire Winfield
Pages 39, 72, 73, 75, 83, 87, 96, 107, 120, 121, 137.